P9-CRZ-367

Reading Matters 3

An Interactive Approach to Reading

Nadia Henein
Mary Lee Wholey

Continuing Education Language Institute
Concordia University

HOUGHTON MIFFLIN COMPANY   Boston   New York

Director, World Languages: Marketing and ESL Publishing   Susan Maguire
Senior Development Editor   Kathleen Sands Boehmer
Editorial Assistant   Manuel Muñoz
Senior Project Editor   Kathryn Dinovo
Senior Cover Design Coordinator   Deborah Azerrad Savona
Senior Manufacturing Coordinator   Priscilla J. Bailey
Marketing Manager   José A. Mercado
Marketing Associate   Claudia Martínez

Cover design and image   Harold Burch, Harold Burch Design, New York City

Photo credits: p. 1: Don Smetzer/Stone; p. 7: Daniel J. Cox/Stone; p. 14: Esbin-Anderson/The Image Works; p. 23: Bachmann/Stock Boston; p. 25: Ellis Herwig/Stock Boston; p. 30: PhotoDisc; p. 45: Myrleen Ferguson/PhotoEdit; p. 53: Ken Fisher/Stone; p. 60: Alison Wright/Stock Boston; p. 70: David Young-Wolff/PhotoEdit; p. 75: Robert Brenner/PhotoEdit; p. 80: Myrleen Ferguson/PhotoEdit; p. 93: J. Greenberg/The Image Works; p. 97: Joe Polillio/Stone; p. 106: Bruce Ayres/Stone; p. 119: Mary C. Etra/PhotoEdit; p. 124L: Peter Cade/Stone; p. 124R: J. Pickerell/The Image Works; p. 132: Hazel Hankin/Stock Boston; p. 135: Kobal Collection; p. 139: Peter Menzel/Stock Boston; p. 141: Fujifotos/The Image Works; p. 144: Courtesy of Probotics; p. 157: David Young-Wolff/PhotoEdit; p. 169: David Young-Wolff/PhotoEdit; p. 181: L. Kolvoord/The Image Works; p. 182: Photofest; p. 184: Bob Daemmrich/Stock Boston; p. 188: Mary Kate Denny/PhotoEdit; p. 195: Jack Olson; p. 198: Quadrillion/Corbis; p. 206: Charles Gupton/Stone; p. 210: Stephen Derr/The Image Bank; p. 215: Najlah Feanny/Stock Boston; p. 219: Steven Rubin/The Image Works; p. 224: J. Berndt/Stock Boston; p. 230: Mark Richards/PhotoEdit; p. 241: David Young-Wolff/PhotoEdit; p. 244: Bonnie Kamin/PhotoEdit; p. 251: Patrick Ramsey/International Stock.

http://college.hmco.com

Printed in the U.S.A.

Library of Congress Catalog Card Number   00-109435

ISBN 0-395-90428-5

23456789-CRS-05 04 03 02 01

As part of Houghton Mifflin's ongoing commitment to the environment, this text has been printed on recycled paper.

Contents

Introduction

The *Reading Matters* series is a four-level reading program comprised of texts at the high beginning/low intermediate, intermediate, high intermediate, and advanced levels. This series combines stimulating readings with well-designed tasks that develop both fluency and accuracy at each level.

Extensive Reading

To develop fluency in reading, students need a significant amount of exposure to text, that is, extensive reading. Extensive reading provides the opportunity to develop automatic text-processing skills. *Reading Matters* offers reading selections of sufficient length so that readers get the chance to increase the amount of time spent in silent reading. Variety in text styles is an important component of extensive reading. The series features a variety of styles and genres so that readers develop an awareness of not only the scope of reading but also the various purposes for which texts are written. Authentic texts or adapted authentic texts are used at appropriate levels.

Intensive Reading

Reading Matters features activities that help students to develop fluency and accuracy in reading by activating two complementary text processing methods: top-down and bottom-up.

TOP-DOWN

Top-down processes are those that the reader applies to understand reading globally. Readers use their background knowledge of the topic and make predictions about what they expect to find out from reading. Readers confirm their predictions and begin to build a mental framework of the information in the reading selection. Awareness of rhetorical patterns, such as chronological ordering, cause and effect, and other discourse features, aids in the comprehension of information from reading. In addition, the activities in *Reading*

Matters help to develop an awareness of a range of reading strategies, such as skimming, scanning, or previewing, that readers have at their disposal. The ability to apply these strategies appropriately is an important component of reading competency.

BOTTOM-UP

Knowledge of grammar and vocabulary has an effect on reading ability. Although readers can predict content from their knowledge of text structure or their background knowledge, a certain level of vocabulary recognition is required for processing text. *Reading Matters* introduces and develops vocabulary-building skills through such activities as guessing from context, recognizing meaning, grouping words, and identifying the use of special terms. In addition to a solid vocabulary, fluent readers have a good knowledge of syntactic structure Actively examining the important grammatical features of a text provides a meaningful context for this kind of learning. To build reading competency, both the amount of exposure to reading and the identification of and practice in the use of learning strategies for both vocabulary and grammar are tremendously important. Reading Matters provides direction to readers through activities in the "Vocabulary Building," "Expanding Your Language," and "Read-On" sections.

Skills Integration and Interaction

Reading is an active process. Interaction between and among students helps facilitate this process. In exchanging ideas about the information in a text, readers confirm what they have understood. This confirmation process helps them develop accuracy in reading. It also provides a motivation for reading, as well as a clear purpose in reading. Interaction with other students can be best accomplished when speaking tasks are an integral part of a reading activity and/or the activity leads to the undertaking of writing tasks.

The interrelationship of skills integration and interaction requires a holistic approach to task design. The activities in *Reading Matters* are sequenced, and the recycling of tasks in various combinations allows the progressive development of reading competency in ways that are fresh and effective. The tasks are structured so that the learner builds skills and strategies progressively but in ways that offer challenge as well as variety. In *Reading Matters,* the reader uses and reuses the language of the selection both implicitly to bolster an answer and explicitly in retelling the reading. Paired reading selections provide complementary or contrasting information on a topic. The readers orally explain the information from the reading they chose to readers who chose a different selection. Then, together, they apply that information to carry out a new activity.

Text Organization

Reading Matters 3 contains six thematic units with two chapters in each unit covering topics related to the themes. Four to five reading selections are featured in each chapter. The unit themes feature topics of high interest to both academically oriented and general audiences. Most important, the selections are of sufficient length for students to progressively develop fluency in reading. Through the chapter readings, students are able to build a rich semantic network without sacrificing variety so that interest in the topic is not exhausted. Within the unit, reading selections are structured so that the information from one selection can be compared with another.

You can choose among the chapters of a unit selectively to suit the needs of different program types and teaching approaches. Complexity in both text type and length and difficulty in task type is structured so that it builds gradually from chapter to chapter and unit to unit. Some overlap in level of language and task is built into each of the texts in the *Reading Matters* series so that you can accommodate the different reading levels of students within a class.

UNIT ORGANIZATION

Each unit in *Reading Matters 3* features the following components:

- "Introducing the Topics," an introductory section that presents the chapter opener photo and quote and offers activities designed to stimulate the readers' curiosity about, prior experience with, or personal relevance of the theme. The tasks are interactive and draw on a variety of media: text, visual, and graphic.

- The two chapters in each unit present topics loosely related to the theme.

CHAPTER ORGANIZATION

For each of the reading selections, the following tasks are presented:

- "Chapter Openers" include prereading reflection and discussion questions, graphs, questionnaires, surveys, or illustrations. The purpose of this section is to stimulate discussion of key ideas and concepts presented in the reading and to introduce key vocabulary. Encourage students to explain their ideas as completely as possible. Teach students strategies for maximizing their interaction, such as turn taking, eliciting responses from all group members, naming a group leader and reporter. Whenever possible, re-form groups to give students a chance to talk more until they feel comfortable with the topic. Elicit key ideas and language from the students.

- "Understanding and Exploring Reading" contains content questions of varying levels of complexity, questions that guide students in the development of their reading strategies for improving general comprehension, for developing an awareness of text structure, and for evaluating the content of a text in detail. Emphasize the purpose of the activity and how it is tied to the development of a particular strategy. It is important to help students build tolerance for uncertainty. Point out that the purpose of comparing and checking their answers with the information in the reading is to give them the opportunity to verify as well as to become familiar with the information. Act as a resource to help students find the accurate information. An answer key is provided to be used when needed.

- "Paired Readings: Recapping, Retelling and Reacting to the Reading" present interactive activities that involve oral presentation of information from the readings, oral exchanges of information, and discussion that involves critical evaluation of ideas including comparison/contrast and debate. Emphasize the importance of explaining the information in as natural and conversational a style as possible. To help students develop their skill at extracting important information from a text, point out the purpose of note taking, highlighting, and underlining key information. Emphasize the importance of practicing at home for in-class presentations.

- "Vocabulary Building" comprises tasks that introduce vocabulary-building strategies such as the understanding of the interrelationship of grammatical structure and meaning, using context cues, and other aids to the fluent processing of reading selections.

- "Expanding Your Language" presents activities that offer students the opportunity to use the material and strategies presented in each selection for the purposes of their own speaking and writing. Encourage students to use these activities to further their own comprehension of the readings. Through these activities students can improve their speaking and writing fluency.

- "Read On: Taking It Further" presents opportunities for personal reading and related activities, including suggestions for further reading as well as reading and writing journal entries, vocabulary logs, and word play. While this work is done outside of class, time can be found in the class schedule to report on some of the activities. This gives students a purpose for the work and practice in developing their reading skills and strategies.

Acknowledgments

We are grateful to Susan Maguire, who first suggested the idea for the series. A special thanks goes to Kathy Sands Boehmer, who has been an invaluable help throughout the lengthy process of bringing this manuscript into its present form. Thanks also to the production and editorial staff at Houghton Mifflin.

Our gratitude to the people who read the manuscript and offered useful suggestion and critical comments: Belinda Adams, Navarro College, TX; Valerie de Carvalho, Pasadena City College, CA; Duffy Galda, Pima Community College, AZ; Barbara Hockman, City College of San Francisco; Roxanne Nuhaily, University of California at San Diego; Barbara Smith-Palinkas, University of South Florida, Tampa; Joan Sears, Texas Tech University; Anne-Marie Schlender, California State University at Hayward.

We would like to acknowledge the support and inspiring work of colleagues and students at the Continuing Education Language Institute (CELI) of Concordia University in Montreal. A special thanks goes to

Adrianne Sklar for her advice and suggestions after reading drafts of the material. The continuing support of Lili Ullmann and Phyllis Vogel has been invaluable to us. Thanks to Devorah Ritter who helped in the preparation of the answer key.

Finally, thanks to our families, Jerry, Jonah, and Yael and Sherif, Ghada, and Dina.

Mary Lee Wholey and Nadia Henein

Reading Matters: Overview

UNIT	SKILLS	ACTIVITIES	VOCABULARY	EXPANSION
UNIT 1 Weather Matters	• brainstorming (1) • previewing (1) • surveying (1) • getting main ideas (1) • understanding details (1) • skimming (1, 2) • scanning for specific information (2) • recapping the information, highlighting (2) • understanding a scientific explanation (2)	• compare and contrast (1) • presenting information in table form (1) • understanding an argument (1) • finding support for an argument (1) • applying information, making a decision (1) • reacting to a point of view (1) • what is your opinion (2) • matching (2) • recapping, reacting to, and retelling information (2) • questionnaire (2) • applying an explanation (2)	• synonymns (1) • using context to guess meaning (1, 2) • adjectives and nouns (2)	• how would you react (1) • newspaper article presentation (1) • reaction writing (1, 2) • free writing (1) • be the expert (2) • report writing (2)
UNIT 2 Fun Matters	• previewing using sidebars (3, 4) • predicting (3) • skimming (3, 4) • scanning for details (3, 4) • getting information from a graph (3) • notetaking, understanding reasons (4) • grouping similar information (4)	• quotations (3) • personalizing (3, 4) • using evidence to support ideas (3) • evaluating information, removing stereotyping (3) • retelling, making a profile (3) • what do you think, true or false (4) • getting information from a chart (4) • using quotes (4)	• using punctuation, commas (3) • colors (4) • parallelism (4)	• interviewing (3) • personal writing (3) • two minute talk (4) • topic writing (4)

Reading Matters: Overview *(continued)*

UNIT	SKILLS	ACTIVITIES	VOCABULARY	EXPANSION
UNIT 3 Time Matters	• understanding facts and opinions (5) • understanding details in a study (6)	• matching meanings (5, 6) • interviews (5) • applying information, solving a problem (6) • giving advice, looking for tips (6)	• word forms (5) • vocabulary in context (5) • matching, general information and specific facts (6) • signal words (6)	• oral presentation (5) • group work, time capsule (5) • topic writing (5) • explaining a different point of view (6) • a sense of humor (6) • managing your time (6)
UNIT 4 Technology Matters	• predicting using knowledge (7) • skimming/tellback (7) • finding main ideas, chunking (7) • scanning, tracing dev't of idea (7) • note taking, finding evidence (7) • Recognizing main ideas, details (7) • using main ideas to scan for details (8)	• analyzing our needs (7) • definitions (7) • giving your opinion (7) • exploring the consequences (7) • applying information, contrasting ideas (8)	• reference words (7) • expressions in context (7, 8)	• debate (7) • talk it out (7) • reaction writing (7, 8) • role play (8) • oral presentation (8)
UNIT 5 Attitude Matters	• paraphrasing (9) • predicting from quotes (10) • inference (10)	• expressions (9) • report on anger studies (9) • debating the issues (9) • charting results (10) • applying information, achieving our goals (10)	• language of examples (9) • word forms, adverbs (10)	• interviewing (9) • journal writing (9, 10) • topic writing (9) • simulation, role play (10)
UNIT 6 Health Matters	• scanning for important information, underlining (11) • analyzing the introduction (12)	• Proverbs (11) • applying the information, making a decision (11) • following a process (12) • analyzing quotes (12)	• expressions in context (11) • using quotes (11) • use of repetitions and synonyms (12) • loaded words (12)	• debate (11) • reaction writing (11) • free writing (11) • analyzing a situation (12) • reacting to a specific situation (12)

Weather Matters

We shall never be content until each man makes his own weather and keeps it to himself.

– Jerome K. Jerome

Introducing the Topics

Weather has always played an important role in our lives. Recently, however, we seem to have started to play a role in the kind of weather we have. In Chapter 1, we will look at what is happening to the weather these days. In Chapter 2, we will look at specific ways in which the weather can affect us.

Points of Interest

DISCUSSION QUESTIONS

Think about these questions. Share your ideas with a partner or in a small group.

1. Check (✔) as many different weather conditions as you know about from the list below.

   _____ windstorms   _____ rainstorms

   _____ thunderstorms   _____ snowstorms

   _____ ice storms   _____ sandstorms

   _____ heat waves   _____ typhoons

   _____ hurricanes

   Which have you experienced? What are the consequences of each?

2. Do you think the weather can have an effect on our health? Our moods? Give examples from your own experiences.

3. Describe the weather conditions you like most or least. Give reasons for your choices.

CHAPTER 1

Our Changing Climate: Reality and Risks

Chapter Openers

A. WHAT'S THE WEATHER NEWS?

Every time we open a newspaper, we find news about the weather. List some common weather terms that you know.

Example: *rainfall*

> *inches of snow*

_____

_____

_____

_____

_____

Some examples of weather reports are given on page 4. Read each one quickly and underline the following:

- Location
- Type of weather
- What happened as a result

Deadly Brazilian Chill

SAO PAULO, BRAZIL–Two people died in southern Brazil from one of the worst cold waves to hit the region in recent history. Up to 5 inches of snow was dumped on some rural areas, but fatalities occurred in the slums of Sao Paolo, where temperatures dropped to 37 degrees Fahrenheit. Temperatures in several communities of the southern state of Rio Grande do Sul dropped to 14 degrees as the region had snowfall for the first time since 1994.

Beaches in Copacabana, Ipanema, and Leblon were deserted due to the frigid conditions.

Camel Drowning

RAJASTHAN, INDIA–At least forty-eight camels drowned in northern India's Rajasthan State due to flash floods triggered by monsoon rains. Incessant rainfall broke an embankment, causing water to gush from the breech and form a huge lake in the Thar Desert.

Belgium Twister

TOURNAI, BELGIUM–A tornado swept through the western Belgian city of Tournai, injuring five people and damaging at least 300 homes and 100 cars. The powerful winds ripped roofs from buildings and smashed windows in the city as well as adjacent villages. The famed twelfth-century cathedral in the historic part of Tournai was not damaged.

B. DISCUSSION QUESTIONS

Using what you underlined, discuss the following questions with a partner or in a small group.

1. What kind of weather conditions do these articles report?
2. What are the consequences in each case?
3. What other damages could have resulted?

C. COMPARE AND CONTRAST

Can the same weather have both good and bad consequences? The following two reports about El Niño were taken from the *same* newspaper. Read them quickly and fill in the table that follows.

El Niño Update

1. As El Niño storms continue to strike several areas of the world, the extent of the damage and death toll in the two hardest-hit countries are just now becoming apparent.

Mudslides and flooding triggered by El Nino in Peru and Ecuador since mid-December have killed at least 300 people and left more than 250,000 others homeless. These figures are double the number of deaths and destruction that occurred during the previous record El Niño, in 1982–83.

In Venezuela, El Niño produced a record heat wave in the normally temperate capital of Caracas, with the temperature soaring to 89 degrees Fahrenheit. Neighboring Colombia is in the midst of a drought because of the ocean-warming phenomenon. The dry spell could cause a drop in production for the country's key coffee export crop.

El Niño's good news

2. It's hard to find any good news resulting from El Niño, but some of the rains that have fallen in Africa are helping to replenish wildlife in the skies and lakes of Kenya. The number of flamingos migrating to waters of Lake Nakuru in the Rift Valley dwindled during recent years. But this season's heavy rains have filled the lake to the brim, and 1.5 million flamingos have returned to feed in its warm, brackish waters.

Mammals have also benefited from the abundance of food created by the rains. Sleek well-fed lions can be seen resting in the low-slung branches of acacia trees near the banks of Nakuru, watching their playful cubs romp in the long grass below.

Consequences

NEGATIVE   POSITIVE

1. _____   1. _____

2. _____   2. _____

3. _____   3. _____

Think of other weather conditions that could be good for some people and bad for others. For example: a heavy snowfall could mean good skiing for some and having to stay home for others.

Exploring and Understanding Reading

Why is the world experiencing such extreme weather conditions? One answer is global warming. However, not everybody agrees about the reasons for global warming or about whether the consequences are good or bad.

BRAINSTORMING

■ *READING TIP:*
Brainstorming: to say or write everything that you know about a topic. It is a useful technique to use before reading because it helps you prepare for the information.

Share what you know about the following with a partner or a small group.

1. What is global warming?
2. Why is it happening?
3. How do we know that it is happening?
4. Which parts of the world are/will be the most affected?

PREVIEWING

■ *READING TIP:*
Previewing is a useful reading skill. One way to preview is to read the title, subtitle(s), and look at the picture(s).

Look at the picture, title, and subtitle of this article. List three ideas you think will be discussed in the reading.

1. _____

2. _____

3. _____

Compare your ideas with a partner.

SURVEYING

■ READING TIP:
Surveying is another useful reading skill. It means to (a) read the introduction, and (b) read the first sentence of every paragraph after that.

Survey the reading. Read the introduction (paragraph 1) and the first sentence of every paragraph after that. Check to see if your preview predictions were correct. If you think you were wrong, change your predictions.

THE NATIONAL POST

Arctic Meltdown

Recent findings add up to a startling conclusion: The Earth's northern ice cap is melting faster than previously thought and could be gone in fewer than 50 years.

By Margaret Munro

1. First came the report from Canadian biologists that polar bears are threatened by starvation because the Arctic season is growing shorter. Then came evidence, gathered by American nuclear submarines prowling Arctic waters, that the ice is 40 percent thinner than it used to be. More recently, Norwegian scientists spying on the Arctic with satellites have come in with a report that the enormous ice sheet that sits atop the planet is shrinking twice as fast as previously thought. The three independent studies, published in prestigious research journals, all point in the same ominous direction: the Arctic ice is shrinking at an unprecedented rate. And if the trend continues, the Arctic could be ice free within decades.

2. Scientists stress it is not clear that the ice-shrinking trend will continue. Most expect the pace will slow down—perhaps even reverse—at least temporarily. But it is hard to know for certain since no one knows what has triggered the big melt, although plenty of scientists think human activities are at least partly responsible. "There is the obvious suspicion it is linked to global warming," says Henry Hengeveld, Environment Canada's senior science adviser on climate change. "There is also the real possibility that it is part of a long-term oscillation back and forth in the Arctic Ocean. A little bit like El Niño, except on a longer time scale."

3. What is clear is that the Arctic has been undergoing remarkable change in the past 30 years. More dramatic change, it appears, than at any time in the last 1,000 years. "All of a sudden we're seeing the ice retreat farther than we've ever seen before," says Hengeveld, who describes the new studies as "startling." "We have evidence that the ice is 40 percent thinner than it was before," he says. "If you add another 20 years and it's another 40 percent thinner, you've really got very little left."

4. The impact of such an "Arctic melt-down" would be incredible. The face of the planet, capped year-round with an ice sheet the size of the United States, would be transformed. Polar bears, seals, and other creatures used to life in the cold would be devastated. Weather patterns across the northern hemisphere would probably change dramatically. People in the Far North would have to face a new reality. "It would change the whole ecology of the system," says Hengeveld.

5. For some Arctic creatures, such as polar bears, the impact has already started to show up in their body fat. A 19-year study by the Canadian Wildlife Service describes how the bears are getting less to eat because the sea-ice season has been reduced annually by 3 weeks. With less time to hunt seals and other food on the ice, the bears are returning to land for the summer months with much less weight to carry them through the ice-free season. While the bears are skinnier than they used to be, the biologists report that the population is still holding its own. But if the warming trend continues, they fear it will not be able to continue alone.

6. Scientists have been aware for years that the Arctic ice pack is getting smaller, but the rate of decline was believed to be about 3 percent a decade, which meant the ice would be around for 300 years or more. But new evidence suggests it is shrinking much faster. Using data collected from satellites, this week a Norwegian team reported that the ice is disappearing at a rate of 7 percent a decade. Their findings, published in the journal *Science*, were based on the amount of multiyear ice, which does not melt in the summer. This ice was measured between 1978 and 1998. The ice pack appears to be undergoing substantial rather than minor changes concludes the Norwegian team led by Ola Johannessen, a polar researcher at the Nansen Environmental and Remote Sensing Centre in Bergen.

7. The Norwegian findings echo recent reports by U.S. scientists who have been going through measurements taken by U.S. nuclear submarines of polar ice thickness. The submarines used acoustic sounds to measure the ice thickness. The data suggest that the ice has thinned from an average of 10.3 feet to about 6 feet, or about 15 percent a decade. And it thinned at every site examined, according to Andrew Holbrook, of the University of Washington in Seattle, who led the team. They say the ice cover that stretches across the top of the globe is about 40 percent thinner than it was two to four decades ago.

8. The lack of historical data makes it difficult for scientists to know just how significant the thinning is. They suspect it is the most that has happened in the last 1,000 years, but they cannot know for sure. Some scientists are saying they believe the changes are the result of global warming. A team of climatologists at the University of Maryland have used satellite information and climate models to support this idea. They made a 5,000-year model of global climate and found that the probability of the present warming trend was less than 2 percent. When they included human-induced changes such as greenhouse gases, the model gave a better match of temperature increases, thus suggesting that the Arctic meltdown could in part be a response to global warming.

9. Environment Canada's Hengeveld remains to be convinced. He worries about the impact of crying wolf. "We have to be careful about being too conclusive about this," he says. "If it is a natural oscillation and the ice starts growing back again, people will say: 'See, global warming is no longer an issue.'" Having said that, he is clearly worried about the Arctic, which at the present rate might be completely ice free in the summer by 2050.

GETTING THE MAIN IDEAS

Write the main idea for each paragraph.

Paragraph 1. *Introduction – important changes in the Arctic*

Paragraph 2. _____

Paragraph 3. _____

Paragraph 4. _____

Paragraph 5. *Study on polar bears*

Paragraph 6. _____

Paragraph 7. _____

Paragraph 8. _____

Paragraph 9. *Conclusion*

Compare your answers with a partner. Then read the text quickly and check your main ideas.

UNDERSTANDING DETAILS

Circle *T* for true and *F* for false. Underline the section in the reading that supports your answer.

1. T F   Three studies have been carried out in the Arctic.

2. T F   The ice shrinking is going to continue.

3. T F   Polar bears are losing weight because they do not have enough time to hunt.

4. T F   The Arctic ice pack is declining at a rate of 3 percent a decade.

5. T F   Some scientists have shown that what is happening in the Arctic is because of global warming.

Check your answers with a partner. If necessary, refer to what you have underlined.

PRESENTING INFORMATION IN TABLE FORM

A few years ago, parts of New England and southern Canada experienced an ice storm that many think was a direct result of global warming. The effects were disastrous because, instead of snow, parts of these regions got freezing rain or ice. The following reading contains different statistics that show the seriousness of the situation.

Read the article quickly and then fill in the tables that follow.

THE GAZETTE

Ice-Storm Numbers Tell Chilling Tale

In January 1998, three successive storms dropped more than 4 inches of freezing rain in areas of New England and southern Canada.

By Terrance Wills

For those who have not lived through an ice storm, 0.2 inches makes driving dangerous, 0.4 inches makes sidewalks treacherous, 1.2 inches can bring down small tree branches, 2.8 inches fells trees and utility poles, and 4 inches can bring down hydroelectric towers. By the time the January 1998 storms were over, more than 4 inches of freezing rain had fallen south of Montreal.

As a result, 1.5 million Canadians encountered between 1.6 and 2.4 inches of freezing rain; another 2.9 million people saw between 2.4 and 3.2 inches collect on their roofs, streets, cars, trees, barns, etc. For nearly 900,000 Canadians, the accumulation was between 3.2 and 4 inches; and for the unluckiest 185,852, the storms deposited more than 4 inches of ice. In all, 5.4 million Canadians—18.7 percent of the country's population—were hit by the three storms.

Some other figures:

- About 100,000 people had to take refuge in shelters, while the Red Cross raised more than $10 million to help victims.

- The ice brought down more than 1,000 power transmission towers and 30,000 wooden utility poles. Nearly 1.7 million customers lost their electricity, in some areas for weeks.

- More than one-third of farming land was struck. Nearly 5.3 million sugar-maple taps were in the path of the storm, and it may take 30 to 40 years for maple syrup production to return to normal.

- The hardest hit were dairy farmers, as nearly one-quarter of Canada's cows were subjected to the storm. The ones that survived may never reach their previous level of production. Furthermore, 2.5 million gallons of milk, valued at more than $5 million, had to be dumped because there was no electricity.

Fill out the following tables based on the reading.

Table 1: General Consequences of Freezing Rain

Amount of rain (inches)	Consequences
0.2	Driving becomes hard
0.4	
1.2	
2.8	
4.0	

Table 2: People Affected

Number of people	Amount of rain (inches)
1.5 million	1.7–2.4
	2.4–3.2
0.9 million	
	> 4.0

Table 3: Damages

Areas	Damages
People	
Electric power	
Crops	
Dairy	

Use the three tables to talk about the ice storm with a partner or in a small group.

UNDERSTANDING AN ARGUMENT

So far we have read about the negative consequences of global warming, but not everybody agrees that it is all bad news. The next article, "What's Wrong with Global Warming?," looks at the situation from a different point of view.

SKIMMING

■ READING TIP:
Skimming is reading an article very quickly just to get a general idea of what it is about.

Read the following statements. Skim the article and put a check mark (✔) beside the statements that are correct. Change the statements that are incorrect. Underline the section in the reading that supports your answer.

_____ a. The author does not believe that global warming is happening.

_____ b. The author believes that global warming might be happening but that it is a positive thing.

_____ c. The author's opinion is based on what happened almost 1,000 years ago.

_____ d. The author believes that there are no negative consequences to global warming.

_____ e. The author shows that many of the predictions made about the future are untrue.

Check your answers with a partner. If necessary, refer to the reading.

What's Wrong with Global Warming?

By Dennis T. Avery

The last time Earth had a balmy era, good things happened.

1. We've all read global warming scare stories. Though some scientists insist there is cause for alarm, evidence indicates otherwise. Global warming may be coming, but if it does, it won't necessarily be extreme. And it might actually be a boon for the environment.

2. Previous computer models were predicting two to three times as much warming as they currently do. Now some researchers say that the Earth is likely to warm by about 3 degrees Fahrenheit during the next century. That may sound like a lot, but it isn't.

3. The world has experienced approximately that much warming fairly recently. And we loved it. Between A.D. 900 and 1300, the Earth warmed by some 3 degrees, according to the Oregon Institute of Science and Medicine. Scholars refer to that period—one of the most favorable in human history—as the Medieval Climate Optimum.

4. Food production surged, many scientists believe, because winters were milder and growing seasons longer. Key agricultural regions experienced fewer floods and droughts. (There was more rainfall, but it evaporated faster.) Death rates declined in many places, partly because of the decrease in hunger and partly because people spent less time in damp, smoke-filled hovels that helped spread tuberculosis and other infectious diseases.

5. Prosperity stimulated an outpouring of creativity in architecture, art, and practical invention. In Europe, artisans built soaring cathedrals. In Southeast Asia, the Khmer people built the huge temple complex of Angkor Wat. The Burmese built thousands of temples at their capital, Pagan. The windmill and spinning wheel entered daily life, while new iron-casting techniques led to better tools.

6. Trade flourished, in part because there were fewer storms at sea. The Vikings discovered Greenland around 950. They were able to support themselves by keeping cattle on what is now frozen tundra. Farming moved north in Scandinavia, Russia, and Japan.

7. We know less about North America. We do know that the Great Plains, the upper Mississippi Valley, and the American Southwest apparently received more rainfall than now. The Anasazi civilization grew abundant irrigated crops and then vanished when the Medieval Optimum ended and rainfall declined. And in North Africa there is some evidence that the Sahara shrank in response to the increase in rain. There were negatives, of course. The steppes of Asia and parts of California, for instance, suffered dry periods. But over all, the medieval experience with global warming should reassure us greatly.

8. The latest evidence supports such optimism, say many scientists. The prospective warming is expected to moderate low nighttime and winter temperatures rather than raise daytime and summer temperature highs. Thus it will produce less added stress on plants, trees, and people.

9. The expected increase in carbon dioxide (CO^2) levels due to the burning of fossil fuels could create a "plant heaven." CO^2 acts as fertilizer for plants. More than a thousand experiments with food crops in twenty-nine different countries show that doubling the world's carbon dioxide would raise crop yields by half. And with an increase in CO^2, forests all over the world should be more robust, allowing them to support more wildlife.

10. Most of the trillion-dollar estimates of global warming costs headlined in the 1980s were based on forecasts that places like New York and Bangladesh would be drowned under rising seas from melting polar ice caps. That frightening scenario, scientists say, is untrue. It may seem paradoxical, but a modest warming in the normally cold and dry polar regions will actually mean more arctic ice, not less. If temperatures warm a few degrees, there will be more moisture in the air, more snowfall, more polar ice.

11. Global warming scaremongers have also claimed that a warmer world could suffer more extreme weather. This, too, is unlikely. According to S. Fred Singer, professor emeritus of Environmental Sciences at the University of Virginia, most of the warming, if it occurs, will be toward the poles. That means there will be less temperature difference between the equator and the poles, which means fewer big storms.

12. History and the science of climatology indicate that we have nothing to worry about. Any global warming in the twenty-first century should be modest, bringing back one of the most pleasant and productive environments humans— and wildlife—have ever enjoyed.

–Reader's Digest

FINDING SUPPORT FOR AN ARGUMENT

Find the information that supports the following statements that the author makes about the past and the future. Underline the information, then write it in your own words in note form. The first one has been done as an example.

■ *READING TIP:*
In English, it is necessary to give support for a point of view. Stating it is not enough. This support can be in the form of an explanation, an example, and statistics. Special words, such as because, for example, *and in other words, are used to introduce support.*

Past

1. The world has already gone through a warm period.

   Between A.D. *900 and 1300 earth warmed by 3 degrees*

2. Food production went up.

   _____

3. Death rates went down.

   _____

4. Architecture improved.

   _____

Future

5. Increase in carbon dioxide levels will be a good thing.

   _____

   _____

6. Flooding will not happen because the polar ice cap will increase rather than decrease.

   _____

   _____

7. A warmer world will not lead to extreme weather conditions.

   _____

   _____

Check your answers with a partner.

After Reading

APPLYING THE INFORMATION: MAKING A DECISION

Is global warming beneficial or not?

Using the readings in the chapter as well as your own knowledge, find reasons for each side of the question. Give support for each reason.

BENEFICIAL	NOT BENEFICIAL
1. _____	1. _____
_____	_____
_____	_____
2. _____	2. _____
_____	_____
_____	_____
3. _____	3. _____
_____	_____
_____	_____

Work with a partner. Compare your reasons. Together, decide whether global warming is beneficial or not and why. Report on your decision to the class.

REACTING TO A POINT OF VIEW

The article "What's Wrong with Global Warming?" presents a very convincing but one-sided argument. It is therefore important to analyze it carefully before we accept everything in it. Use the following questions to analyze the article. Share your answers with a partner or with a small group.

1. Does the author give a complete picture of what the consequences of global warming will be? If not, what is missing?

2. Is it reasonable to expect what happened 1,000 years ago to happen again in the future? Why? Why not?

3. According to the author, an increase in carbon dioxide could create a "plant heaven." That is good, but what else do you think might happen?

Discuss whether or not you still find the argument in favor of global warming convincing. Share your ideas with the class.

Vocabulary Building

SYNONYMS

READING TIP:
When you are writing about a certain topic, some ideas or concepts may come up repeatedly. It is boring to use the same words over and over again. That is why synonyms are very important.

Refer to "Ice Storm Numbers Tell Chilling Tale" to find the words in context. Match the words in Column A with words that have the same meaning in Column B.

Column A

_____ 1. treacherous

_____ 2. dumped

_____ 3. fells

_____ 4. struck

_____ 5. freezing rain

_____ 6. accumulation

Column B

a. ice

b. brings down

c. total rainfall

d. dangerous

e. dropped

f. hit

VOCABULARY IN CONTEXT

Words you already know can help you understand the meaning of a new word. Circle the words that help you guess the meaning of the word in boldface. Write your definition of the word. Then consult a dictionary to check your definition.

1. Global warming may be coming, but if it does, it won't necessarily be extreme. And it might be a **boon** for the environment.

   _____

2. Food production **surged**, many scientists believe, because growing seasons were longer. _____

3. In North Africa there is some evidence that the Sahara **shrank** in response to the increase in rain. _____

4. CO^2 acts as **fertilizer** for plants. Experiments with food crops show that doubling the world's carbon dioxide would raise crop yields by half. _____

5. It may seem **paradoxical**, but some warming in the cold and dry polar regions will mean more ice, not less.

   _____

6. Global warming **scaremongers** have also claimed that a warmer world could have more extreme weather.

   _____

7. No one is sure what has **triggered** the big ice melt.

   _____

8. The ice pack appears to be undergoing **substantial** rather than minor changes. _____

Check your answers. Work with a partner and take turns reading your sentences.

Expanding Your Language

SPEAKING

A. How Would You React? Work with two to three classmates. Try to imagine the situation described in "Ice Storm Numbers Tell Chilling Tale." The following might help:

- The city of Montreal has a population of about 2 million. At one point almost 90 percent were without electricity.
- A few days after the storm, the temperature dropped to about minus 5 degrees Fahrenheit.
- Trees, telephone lines, power lines, and poles had fallen everywhere: across streets, on rooftops, on cars.

Some resulting scenarios are described in the following statements. Read each one and discuss your answers to the question that follows it.

- Temperatures inside houses dropped to below the freezing point, yet many people refused to leave their homes.
  What do you think was the reason for that?
- When they were forced to leave, they had the choice of going either to shelters or to friends who had power.
  What do you think they chose and why?
- Firewood and generators became very scarce.
  What do you think happened as a result?
- Schools were closed for two weeks.
  How do you think children reacted?
- Despite all the discomfort and fear and anxiety, many people have very positive feelings about the storm.
  Why is that?

B. Newspaper Article Presentation:

1. Read the following article and use the information to answer these questions.

- How are people causing it to rain?
- Do you think the evidence supports the conclusion?
- Are you surprised?

THE GLOBE AND MAIL

People May Drive Weather Patterns

Car exhaust a culprit in rainy weekends

By Steven Strauss

How many times have you heard someone complain that the weather is beautiful during the week but crummy during the weekend?

Well, according to a new U.S. study, people and their pollutant-spewing cars are helping to create that weather pattern.

Using weather and pollutant measurements, climatologists Randall Cerveny and Robert Balling at Arizona State University are publishing a paper in *Nature* magazine that outlines a seven-day weather cycle.

The cycle annually produces 22 percent more rain on Saturdays than on Mondays over the East Coast of Canada and the United States. On average, Mondays, Tuesdays, and Wednesdays are consistently drier than the weekends.

"We think this is an artifact of man and is not found in nature," Prof. Cerveny said. He argues that the culprit is well-documented changes in the emission levels of nitrogen oxides in motor vehicle exhaust.

David Parrish, a chemist with the National Oceanic and Atmospheric Administration in Boulder, Colorado, said North American figures show that emissions of the offending oxides diminish by 17 percent on weekends. This is thought mainly to reflect work-related changes in driving patterns on weekends. Some of the information used to arrive at this conclusion was collected at Sable Island off the coast of Nova Scotia and at Cape Race in Newfoundland. These places are directly in the path of wind-borne pollutants from heavily populated regions.

The two Arizona climatologists argue in their paper that it is easy to construct a scenario where variations in car pollutants could trigger large-scale climate changes. For example, it is known that the small particles found in exhaust fumes absorb heat and subsequently heat the air around them.

"A fundamental principle of meteorology is that warm air rises and, as it rises, it is more likely to create clouds and rainfall," Prof. Cerveny said.

The paper presents a series of statistical correlations to make its case. For example, in the mid-Atlantic, the increased rainfall occurs on Wednesdays—consistent with the time it would take for winds to carry the pollutants there. The rainfall increase in the Atlantic is also smaller than that recorded near the more polluted mainland.

"It is definitely an intriguing statistical connection, but a lot more work needs to be done," says Dr. Parrish, one of the study's referees.

2. Check your local newspaper for the next few days. Find an interesting article on some aspect of the weather. Prepare to talk about it by doing the following things.

a. Skimming: Quickly read the article to get the general idea and to check whether or not the information is interesting.

b. Highlighting: Think of three ideas that the article discusses and highlight information about each.

c. Practice your presentation using the highlighted information.

d. Present your information.

e. Comment on why you found it interesting.

WRITING

Reaction Writing: Write what you think about one of the following ideas.

▪ **READING TIP:**
It is useful to have a separate folder in which you can keep all the writing that you do in each chapter.

1. The statement "One day we will be able to control the weather."

2. A time when the weather prevented you from doing something you really wanted to do

3. A time when the weather caused major problems in your city/town/country

CHAPTER 2

A SAD Situation

Chapter Openers

Beat the Winter Blues . . .

The Tropics Are Calling!

WHAT IS YOUR OPINION? AGREE OR DISAGREE

Circle *A* if you agree or *D* if you disagree with the statement.

1. A   D   The psychological effects of weather have a greater impact on people than the physical effects do.

2. A   D   People who say they are depressed because of the weather are just looking for an excuse.

3. A   D   The effect of the weather on our health is greater now than it was in the past.

Compare your answers with a partner or a small group. Give reasons or examples to support your opinion.

MATCHING

A. Work with a partner. Match the following conditions with the definitions below.

Conditions

1. _____ migraine headaches   4. _____ asthma

2. _____ allergies   5. _____ depression

3. _____ the flu   6. _____ arthritis

Definitions

a. Lung disease that causes tightness of the chest, coughing and difficulty breathing.

b. An unusual physical reaction to certain foods or substances

c. A disease that causes inflammation and stiffness in the joints of the body.

d. The condition of feeling sad and sorrowful.

e. A very severe headache that usually affects one side of the head and tends to happen repeatedly.

f. A contagious viral disease that causes fever, inflammation of the respiratory system, and muscle pain.

B. Check (✔) the conditions you think are related to the weather. Explain the connection between the conditions you checked and the weather.

PAIRED READING

People have known for a long time that some psychiatric (or mental) disorders are somehow related to changes in seasons. The readings that follow are about two such disorders: Reading 1 is about SAD (Seasonal Affective Disorder) and Reading 2 "Sad in the Sunshine" is about Reverse SAD. Choose one of these readings. Work with a partner who is reading the *same* article.

SKIMMING

Quickly skim the article and answer the following questions.

■ *READING TIP:*
Skimming allows you to get a general idea of what an article is about. When you skim, read quickly; focus on ideas that you understand.

1. At what time of the year does this disorder happen?

   _____

2. How does this disorder make people feel?

   _____

Reading 1: Seasonal Affective Disorder (SAD)

Seasonal Affective Disorder (SAD)

By Gila Lindsley, Ph.D., A.C.P.

As the last of the leaves fall from the trees and the sun sinks lower and lower on the horizon, the spirits of some sink with it; and as the days grow shorter and shorter, many become SAD. That is, many may develop *Seasonal Affective Disorder* (SAD).

1. For those who become SAD with the coming of the cold, dark months, the consequences can be very severe. I'll never forget the first patients I saw with severe SAD. It was in the winter of 1987 or 1988. I was running a Sleep Disorders Center in a New Hampshire psychiatric hospital and had become very interested in SAD as well. The first patient was a woman who was thirty-five or so. She had tried to commit suicide and almost succeeded. I was shaken. I had not realized until then that SAD could be so life threatening. When I talked to her, I found out that she felt SAD every winter, but generally was able to hang on until her kids' February vacation from school, when the family took a vacation in sunny Florida. That immediately lifted her spirits. "What happened this year?" I asked her. "February vacation did not come until the first week of March. I could not hold out any longer." We treated her with several sessions a day of bright light. The difference was amazing. We noticed that her room became unusually full of people during the light sessions.

2. Another patient was a man in his mid-twenties. He was admitted to this same hospital year after year, generally for several months at a time, so severe was his depression. When we looked back at his history, we realized he always came in more or less the same time of year, usually late September, and then was well enough to go home some weeks beyond New Year's Day. He told us that at other times of the year he was just fine. We also exposed him to artificial light. At first he became more sociable. Then he began to pay better attention to personal hygiene, caring to change his clothes, to bathe himself, and to shave.

3. Winter depressions can be very, very severe. Even if not severe enough to require hospitalization, as was the case for these two people, the psychological and physical symptoms can still be severe enough to disturb how you function and perhaps even interfere with your personal relationships.

4. Mood certainly changes. Some people become sad to the point of experiencing real grief at times. Others become more anxious; still others become more irritable. At times the irritability can be so extreme that feelings of violence erupt. This may be one small part of the reason why the incidence of child abuse seems to increase during the dark months.

5. Physical activity decreases. The person feels very lazy, often sluggish. Physical effort of almost any sort seems to be just too much. On the other hand, appetite—especially a craving for carbohydrates (sugars or starches or alcohol)—actually increases. Hypersomnia can develop: most people with SAD end up sleeping for very long hours (or wishing they could, if life would allow it). In many ways, it is as if a person were hibernating during the cold, dark months.

6. Scientists now think that SAD is a result of the decreasing hours of daylight. One of the first studies was done by South African psychiatrist Norman Rosenthal and his colleagues. The investigators found they could predict how many of the people they studied would develop SAD symptoms on the basis of how brief the daylight hours were. As daylight began noticeably decreasing in September, some people were affected. By the time the days close to winter solstice came, almost everyone in the study group was affected. Then, as the season moved away from the solstice toward spring, with lengthening daylight hours, the number of affected people began to decline. By the end of May, almost all were back to their old selves, some unfortunately even switching into what psychiatrists call mania.

7. To make sure that this connection between change in mood and amount of light was more than just chance, the next step was to supply light to see if it could reverse the SAD mood. Rosenthal's team used two different kinds of light. The dimmer, yellow light had no effect. However, the brighter light that resembled actual sunlight produced a marked change in mood in most (but not all) the patients who received that treatment.

–New Technology Publishing Inc.

SCANNING FOR SPECIFIC INFORMATION

Look back to the reading for the answers to these questions. Write your answers in note form.

1. a. Why was the first patient admitted to the hospital?

   _____

   _____

   b. What made her situation worse this year?

   _____

   _____

2. What effect did the light treatment have on the second patient?

   _____

   _____

3. a. Name three psychological symptoms of SAD.

   _____, _____, _____

   b. What can these symptoms lead to?

   _____

4. Name three physical symptoms.

   _____, _____, _____

5. a. According to the study, when do people start getting SAD symptoms?

   _____

   b. How long can these symptoms last?

   _____

6. a. How many kinds of light did the researchers use to treat the patients?

_____

b. Which kind worked? Why?

_____

_____

Compare your answers with your partner's. Try to agree on the same answer. Look back at the reading if you disagree.

RECAPPING THE INFORMATION: HIGHLIGHTING

■ *READING TIP:*
Highlighting is a useful strategy for finding and remembering facts and important ideas you read. To highlight, use a colored highlighting pen to mark information. Be careful to mark only the words and phrases that you want to stand out—not the whole sentence.

A. Highlight the facts you read about SAD that relate to these ideas:

1. SAD patients
2. Symptoms of SAD
3. Study to show that SAD is a result of lack of light

B. Working with a partner, compare what you highlighted. Discuss whether you highlighted too much or too little. Add any highlighting you need to.

C. Using *only* what you highlighted, take turns telling each other the important information in the article. Make sure you explain the information and add any ideas of your own.

REACTING TO THE INFORMATION

Discuss these questions with your partner.

1. Give examples of how having SAD can affect a person's personal relationships.
2. People who have SAD feel very tired and depressed. Which do you think comes first: the depression or the feeling of being tired?
3. What do you think is the explanation for the link between light and symptoms that SAD people have?

Reading 2: SAD in the Sunshine

THE GAZETTE

SAD in the Sunshine

Disorder sufferers find good weather depressing.

By David Johnston

1. As she drove to the mall this week, Audrey Greenway looked up at the strong late-winter sun and groaned. "I took an amphetamine pill this morning because I could see it was turning into a bad day," she said. "The sun was shining, it was pure agony."

2. Greenway, 51, has Reverse Seasonal Affective Disorder. As its name implies, this is the opposite of Seasonal Affective Disorder (SAD), or winter depression.

Greenway suffers from summer depression. Daylight and warmth are factors. Her mental health begins to deteriorate in the spring. For reasons doctors don't understand, Reverse SAD is more debilitating than SAD. It's also more rare. While 4 to 8 percent of us may suffer from SAD, only .025 percent are believed to suffer from the deeper depressions of Reverse SAD. In Greenway's case, Reverse SAD provokes severe manic depression. Her mania (extreme excitement) happens in winter. With the coming of spring, however, she gradually withdraws from social contact and falls into a depression for which she sometimes takes twenty-seven pills a day.

3. Greenway is very open about her illness. She has told her story on video for hospital researchers. Her doctor is encouraging her to speak to women's groups about seasonal depression because women are twice as likely to be depressed as men, studies suggest, and four times as likely to suffer from depressions that follow a seasonal pattern.

4. On the way to the mall, Greenway was upbeat. But as she walked from the parking lot to the doors, her pace slowed. "I feel terrible," she said as she stepped inside the mall. "My body feels like lead. I'm dragging 124 pounds, but it feels like 600. I feel I don't want to be here. My heart is pumping."

5. Though she lives nearby, Greenway usually shops at a mall that is much farther away because it is the "darkest mall in the city." She pointed to this mall's skylights, then at some indoor trees. "The lights, the trees. They bother me."

6. Greenway came to this mall only to buy her mother-in-law a present at a special jewelry store. In December and January, when days are shortest, she enjoys shopping—especially on cold nights. Sometimes she enjoys it too much. Her mania provokes expensive shopping. "I've bought truckloads of curtains." On her doctor's advice, she doesn't keep credit cards in her purse. Still, her husband, Ray, sees to it she has two bank accounts—one for when she is manic, the other for when she is not. "When I'm manic, I'm not supposed to touch the nonmanic account," said Greenway. "But this winter, I touched both." She smiled. "Emptied them out."

7. As she approached the jewelry store, her mood suddenly turned fierce. "I can't stand to see these people," she said of the shoppers walking through the mall. "I'd rather be home in bed. I have to make a decision [on what to buy her mother-in-law] and it is impossible. Depression simply does not allow decisions." She spotted a bench. "Here, I have to sit down first." When she sat down, she started to cry. "People are smiling. Don't they know how much it hurts?" She stopped crying, "I don't envy them. What God gave me—there's some good in it, too. I've become a more patient and gentle person. Still, it hurts. I dread clocks moving forward one hour in spring." She looked up at the jewelry store, wiped her eyes and laughed.

"You'd think I was going for surgery the way I'm behaving."

8. In the store, a saleswoman showed her three varieties of the item she wanted. Greenway chose the first piece. "If I have to make a decision, I'm afraid I might just walk out with nothing," she explained.

9. As she left the store, the newspaper reporter she had invited to tag along asked whether she would like a coffee. She said she would.

"Where would you like to go?"

"A restaurant with no windows."

10. She laughed. "My husband says I know all the dark corners in the city." In the restaurant, Greenway chose the darkest spot she could find, even though artificial light doesn't bother her. In five minutes she had brightened considerably. "I really feel I shouldn't hide all I am going through," she said. "When I talk to women, they say, 'Shh! You shouldn't say that.' We have the wrong impression of mental illness. Five percent of all mental illness is manic depression. And ten of every hundred people will experience in their lives a time of deep depression. So why shouldn't we talk about it?"

SCANNING FOR SPECIFIC INFORMATION

Look back to the reading for the answers to these questions. Write your answers in note form.

1. What kind of medication does Audrey take for her problem?

   _____

2. Compare the number of people who suffer from Reverse SAD to the number of those who suffer from SAD.

   _____

   _____

3. Who does Audrey talk to about her disorder? Why?

   _____

   _____

4. What kinds of malls does she usually shop at? Why?

   _____

   _____

5. a. What happens to Audrey's shopping habits in winter?

      _____

      _____

   b. What advice does her doctor give her about this?

      _____

      _____

   c. What is her husband's solution to this?

      _____

      _____

6. Audrey feels that there is some good in her problem. What is it?

   _____

   _____

7. a. How do people react when Audrey talks about her problem?

      _____

      _____

   b. What is her response?

      _____

      _____

RECAPPING THE INFORMATION: HIGHLIGHTING

A. Highlight the facts in the reading that relate to these ideas:

■ **READING TIP:**
See page 29 for tips
on highlighting.

1. General information on Reverse SAD
2. Effect of Reverse SAD on Audrey's behavior
3. How Audrey deals with her problem

B. Working with a partner, compare what you highlighted. Discuss whether you highlighted too much or too little. Add any highlighting you need to.

C. Using *only* what you highlighted, take turns telling each other the important information in the article. Make sure you explain the information and add any ideas of your own.

REACTING TO THE INFORMATION

Discuss these questions with your partner.

1. How do you think Audrey's condition affects her relationship with her husband and friends?
2. Why would it be useful for her to talk about her problem to other women?
3. What do you think is the explanation for the link between light and symptoms that Reverse SAD people have?

After Reading

RETELLING THE INFORMATION

Work with a partner who read a different article. Use what you highlighted to retell the information. Explain the ideas clearly in your own words. Encourage your partner to ask questions about the information or write some of the important facts you explain. After you have finished retelling, discuss the questions in the preceding section, "Reacting to the Information."

REACTING TO THE READINGS

Keeping in mind the information in both readings and your own experience, share your ideas about these questions:

1. Which condition appears to be worse: SAD or Reverse SAD? Why?
2. Why do you think women are more likely than men to have seasonal disorders?
3. According to Audrey (in Reading 2), people say "Shh! You shouldn't say that," when she talks about her condition. Do you agree with them? Why? Why not?
4. Do you or any one you know suffer from SAD or Reverse SAD?

QUESTIONNAIRE

Answer the following questionnaire to confirm your answer to question 4 in the preceding section.

	Yes	*No*	*Sometimes*
1. Does work and family life become more difficult for you every winter?			
2. Do you experience constant fatigue or periods of fatigue in winter but not in summer?			
3. Do your eating habits change in winter, with more sweet or starch in your diet?			
4. Does your general feeling of well-being tend to decline in the winter?			
5. Do you usually feel fine—or even energized—in late spring and summer without underlying feelings of depression?			

Discuss your results with a partner or in a small group.

UNDERSTANDING A SCIENTIFIC EXPLANATION

Scientists are always trying to explain what they observe. They do this by asking one question after another until they have a complete picture. The following reading is about the questions that scientists have asked about SAD and what they have found out so far.

Work with a partner. Read the answer to the first question. Discuss the information with your partner. Take turns doing the same with the remaining questions.

■ *READING TIP:*
Tellback is a useful technique when reading material that is unfamiliar or a little hard. It means reading a small section and then talking about it <u>without</u> looking back at it.

The Biological Clock

By Gila Lindsley, Ph.D., A.C.P.

Which comes first: feeling depressed or feeling tired?

According to research, the first thing that changes with bright light treatment is energy level. People begin to report feeling less sluggish and less tired, and soon after they report having more energy. Only after this has occurred, does the actual depression begin to lift. Working backwards, we began to think that the depression is a result of feeling tired and not being able to function properly. And so this turns us once again to light, but with a different kind of question.

What does light have to do with sleepiness and sluggishness?

Here is our current understanding. We are biological creatures, and in general the human race depends a great deal on being able to see. When primates and

then humans were evolving, before electricity was discovered, and also before the discovery of fire, we could not see well when it was dark out. That was the time, then, to sleep so one's batteries could be recharged by sunrise for the next day's hunting and gathering. Therefore we must have developed internal biological clocks that are synchronized to the light-dark cycle in the physical world so that we'd be alert by daylight and become sleepy as the sun began to set.

Where is that internal biological clock?

In recent years, a small cluster of brain cells (i.e., neurons) has been identified as where this master biological clock is. It lies right above an important part of the visual system. One kind of information this "clock" receives has to do with the amount of light coming in through the eyes.

What does the clock do with the information it receives about the amount of light or darkness?

It sends it to a gland at the base of the brain called the pineal gland. This gland releases a hormone, melatonin, into the bloodstream. The amount of light seems to determine how much melatonin is released into the bloodstream. With more light, less melatonin is released; and with less light, more melatonin is released.

What does that mean for the changing seasons?

During those seasons when the light periods are long, in the spring and summer, melatonin release is at its lowest since there are fewer hours of darkness. On the other hand, the closer we move toward the winter solstice, the fewer hours of light there are each day and, correspondingly, the longer the period of time each day when melatonin can be released into the bloodstream.

Once melatonin is in the bloodstream, what is the result?

There are no clear answers right now, for this is quite a new field of research. However, one result found over and over again is that melatonin indirectly causes body temperature to drop. We also know that when we fall asleep, our body temperature drops as well. The answer could be that as it gets dark, melatonin is released, causing our body temperature to drop. This then causes us to feel sleepy. A perfect system for prehistoric humans but not for modern times. Maybe that is why a lot of us find it harder to get up early in winter.

What we still need to find out is why some people—i.e. those who have SAD—are so much more affected than others.

–**New Technology Publishing Inc.**

SCANNING FOR DETAILS: REORDERING INFORMATION

The following statements all deal with what happens during dark periods. Read the statements and number them according to the order in which they take place.

_____ a. Clock sends information to the pineal gland.

_____ b. We feel tired and sleepy.

_____ c. Signal about lack of light goes to internal clock.

_____ d. Body temperature goes down.

_____ e. Pineal gland releases melatonin into blood.

Work with a partner to compare the order of the sentences.
Locate and underline the information in the article that matches
the statements.

Write out what happens during periods of light.

a. _____

b. _____

c. _____

d. _____

e. _____

Compare your answers with a partner's.

APPLYING THE EXPLANATION

Work with a partner or in a small group. Discuss whether the
concept of an internal biological clock can be used to explain the
following:

1. Reverse SAD
2. Feeling hungry in the middle of the night
3. Heart attacks happen more often in midmorning.
4. Jet lag
5. We are more likely to feel pain in the morning.

One solution for SAD is to expose the person to bright light for a
certain number of hours every day. Again, based on what you
have read, try to think of possible solutions for the following.

■ Reverse SAD
■ Jet lag

▌ Vocabulary Building

ADJECTIVES AND NOUNS

In English, the form of the word can change when it is used as a different part of speech. For example, a suffix (ending) can be added to change the adjective *sad* to the noun *sadness*. Some common noun suffixes are *-ness, -tion, -ment, -th, -y*.

Choose the correct form of the word for each of the following sentences. In the parentheses ( ), write which part of speech, noun (n) or adjective (adj), is needed to complete the sentence.

1. depressed/depression

    a. In Audrey's case, Reverse SAD causes severe _____ ( ).

    b. Researchers noticed that as the day gets shorter, some people become more _____( ).

2. ill/illness

    a. Greenway is very open about her _____( ).

    b. I got up this morning, took one look at the bright sunlight, and felt quite _____( ).

3. warm/warmth

    a. Malls can become very _____( ) in summer because of all the modern skylights.

    b. Daylight and _____( ) are some of the factors that lead to certain disorders.

4. biological/biology

    a. _____( ) never used to be one of my favorite subjects at school.

    b. Scientists are still trying to find a complete _____ ( ) explanation for Reverse SAD.

VOCABULARY IN CONTEXT

You can often understand the meaning of a new word from your understanding of the other words in a sentence. Match the highlighted word in each sentence with one of the words in the following list.

1. appear suddenly	4. follow after	7. strong desire
2. disturbed	5. weakening	8. fear
3. continue	6. causes	9. get worse

a. _____ Her mental health begins to **deteriorate** in the spring.

b. _____ Reverse SAD is more **debilitating** than SAD.

c. _____ In Audrey's case, Reverse SAD **provokes** severe depression.

d. _____ "I **dread** clocks moving forward in the spring."

e. _____ The newspaper reporter she had asked to **tag along** asked whether she would like a coffee.

f. _____ I was **shaken** when I realized that she had tried to commit suicide.

g. _____ At times the irritability can be so extreme that feelings of violence can **erupt**.

h. _____ She felt SAD every winter but was generally able to **hang on** until a vacation in Florida in February.

i. _____ Appetite and a **craving** for sweets actually increase while a person is suffering from SAD.

Check your answers with a partner or with your teacher.

Expanding Your Language

SPEAKING

Be the Expert: Work with a partner who read a different article. One person takes the role of a reporter. The other takes the role of someone suffering from SAD or Reverse SAD. Interview each other using the following steps.

1. Brainstorm four or five questions you could ask.
   Examples: What disorder do you suffer from?
                  In what way does it affect your life?

2. Use your questions to interview your partner.

3. Make notes on the answers you get.

4. Reverse your roles and repeat steps 1–3.

WRITING

Report Writing: Write a report about your interview. Use these steps to help you.

1. Read over the notes you made during your interview. Make sure you understand them. If necessary, check the information with the person you interviewed.
2. Write a short introduction in which you mention who you are talking to and why.
3. Using the notes you made, write two to three sentences about each answer.
4. Write a short conclusion in which you can give your opinion about the problem.

Reaction Writing: Write what you think about one of the following ideas:

1. When people are affected by the weather, what kind of reactions do they have?
2. Is the effect of the weather on our health greater now than in the past? What will it be like in the future?

Read On: Taking It Further

Researchers have found that the more you read, the more your vocabulary will increase and the more you will understand. A good knowledge of vocabulary will help you to do well in school and in business. To find out more about making reading a habit for yourself, answer the following questionnaire.

READING QUESTIONNAIRE

Rank the activities that you think help you to increase the language you understand. Mark (*1*) beside the one that helps you the most when learning a new language, (*2*) beside the second, and so on. Mark the same number if you find two activities that help you equally.

( ) Memorizing word lists

( ) Reading texts that are assigned for class

( ) Reading texts that I choose for myself

( ) Talking about the texts that we read for class

( ) Talking about the texts that I choose for myself

( ) Learning how to guess the meanings of words that are new

( ) Doing vocabulary exercises for readings that we study in class

( ) Doing extra vocabulary exercises for homework

( ) Studying the dictionary to find out the parts of words

( ) Using the dictionary to look up new words I don't understand

Discuss your questionnaire with a partner. Do not change your answers. Explain the reasons for your ranking and your experiences with reading. Are there other activities that you find help you to increase your vocabulary? Explain what these are and how they help you.

A READING JOURNAL

■ **READING TIP:**
Keep a notebook to write your reading journal and vocabulary log entries.

An important way to improve your reading skills and increase your vocabulary is to find material that you choose to read. This activity is called "reading for pleasure." Here are some ideas to start you out.

Reading

Find some readings on the topics in this unit that you are interested in and that are at your level. Your teacher can help you to find some stories to read for your pleasure. For example, you could read *The Wizard of Oz* in which the heroine, Dorothy, is transported by a cyclone to another world.

Another source of reading material is your bookstore or library's magazine and newspaper section. Discuss what you would like to read with others in a small group. Your group members could recommend something good for you to read. Try to work with a reading partner. Select a reading that your partner or partners will read as well. Make a schedule for the times when you plan to do your personal reading and a time when you would like to finish.

Writing

At the end of each week, complete a journal report about what you read. Explain the important ideas and what you learned from this reading. Write about what you liked or found interesting. Explain whether or not you would recommend the reading to others.

Speaking

Each week, be ready to talk about what you read with a partner or with others in a small group. You can use your journal report to help you to recall what is important for the others to know.

Reading Journal Report

Include the following information in your journal entry:

Title of the reading: _____

Author: _____

Subject of the reading:

_____

_____

_____

_____

Summary of the important ideas:

_____

_____

_____

_____

Personal reaction:

_____

_____

_____

_____

Recommendation:

_____

_____

_____

Vocabulary Log

Choose five important words that you learned from each chapter. Write the words and a definition in your notebook. Check your definition with the teacher.

Example:

Chapter 1	*Word*	*Definition*
1.	symptoms	signs of disorder or disease
2.		
3.		
4.		
5.		

2

Fun Matters

One-half of the world cannot understand the pleasures of the other.

– Jane Austen

Introducing the Topics

To relax and have fun is a very important part of life. The way we do it, however, varies from age to age and culture to culture. This unit is about how our concept of leisure has changed and about the kinds of activities that are becoming more popular these days.

Points of Interest

QUOTATIONS

Read the following quotations. Decide whether they support the idea of leisure, are against the idea of leisure, or are neutral.

Check (✔) the category you decide on.

	For	*Against*	*Neutral*
1. "Pleasure is the object, the duty and the goal of all rational creatures."	_____	_____	_____
2. "There are toys for all ages."	_____	_____	_____
3. "Play so that you may be serious."	_____	_____	_____
4. "It is a good talent to know how to play."	_____	_____	_____
5. "More free time means more time to waste."	_____	_____	_____
6. "In our play, we reveal what kind of people we are."	_____	_____	_____

Work with a partner. Explain what each quote means and try to agree on the best category for each. Discuss whether or not you agree with the quote, and give reasons for your opinion.

QUESTIONNAIRE

Read the following list of reasons for taking time off. Check (✔) the ones that are important to you. Mark their order of importance from *1* (very important) to *5* (least important). Add any ideas of your own.

Reasons to take time off	*Importance*
_____ To have time with family and friends	_____
_____ To be more efficient at work	_____
_____ To improve the economy	_____
_____ To stay healthy	_____
_____ To give others a chance to work	_____
_____ To learn something new	_____
Other: _____	_____

Discuss your list with a partner or in a small group.

Extreme Sports

Chapter Openers

DISCUSSION QUESTIONS

Think about these questions. Share your ideas with a partner or with a small group.

1. What does "taking a risk" mean?
2. What are the characteristics of risk takers?
3. Why do you think that the number of people participating in risky activities is increasing?
4. Is it important to take risks?

PERSONALIZING

Look at the following list of sports. Ask your teacher to explain any that you do not understand. Check *T* for the ones you have tried, check *WLT* for the ones you would like to try, and check *WNT* for the ones you would never think of trying.

	T	WLT	WNT
Alpine skiing			
Rock climbing			
Skydiving			
Wild water rafting			
Snowboarding			
Race car driving			
Deep sea diving			
Bungee jumping			

Work with a partner or in a small group.

- Describe the activities you checked in the *T* column and say what you liked about them.
- Explain why you want to try the activities in the *WLT* column.
- Give reasons for not wanting to try the activities in the *WNT* column.

Exploring and Understanding Reading

PREVIEWING: READING SIDEBARS

The following sidebars are taken from an article on extreme sports.

■ **READING TIP:**
In addition to looking at the pictures and reading the title and subtitle, previewing includes reading sidebars whenever they are included.

Work with a partner.

A. Read each one quickly and take turns telling what each is about.

Mountaineer

I don't remember much about the night I spent alone at Seven Gables in the John Muir Wilderness after falling 100 feet. I was hungry and cold. And I had no feelings in my legs. Since then I've been in this wheelchair for 17 years. At first I lay in the hospital feeling sorry for myself. I couldn't see anything positive. Then I began climbing again with customized gear. I'm the first person to climb the 3,000-foot face of Yosemite's El Capitan and the first paraplegic to ski across the Sierra Nevada.

Pro Snowboarder

Every day I get to do something bigger and better than I've ever done. Like taking a trick and going an extra 15 feet bigger. Of course I'm scared. I don't want to rag doll and hurt myself—that's where I have to conquer my fear. And kids totally respond to that risk taking as part of the appeal. When you go out and try something that's a little bit risky, you feel great about yourself at the end of the day. Because if you're a pro snowboarder and you don't get hurt, then you're not trying hard enough. I've had two knee surgeries, my latest three months ago. But I do what I do because I want to enjoy life to the max.

Walk Up the Wild Side

Most kids who get locked out of the house wait around for Mom and Dad to get home. Ten-year-old Alain Robert scaled his family's seven-story apartment building near Paris and climbed in a window. Twenty-five years later the 5-foot 4-inch, 105-pound urban mountaineer known as Spiderman has climbed buildings including the Empire State Building, the 1,482-foot Petronas Towers in Malaysia, and Chicago's 1,454-foot Sears Tower—all without a rope or any other tools. Robert, who has been jailed on four continents for his illegal climbing, spent his teen years perfecting his skills on the cliffs in the south of France. The only climbing aids he uses are rubber-soled shoes and talcum powder for his hands. Dangerous? Sure, but as Robert sees it, "You are born to die one day . . . I prefer to die in action."

B. Answer the following questions together.

1. What qualities/characteristics do these people have?
2. How do they feel about what they do?
3. How do they handle their fear?

PREDICTING

Using your previewing to help you, list four ideas that you think you will find in the article.

1. _____

2. _____

3. _____

4. _____

Compare your ideas with a partner.

SKIMMING

A. Read the article quickly and add to or change your predicted ideas.

B. Answer the question that is asked in the subtitle: Why are Americans seeking risk as never before?

Life on the Edge

By Karl Taro Greenfield

Why are Americans seeking risk as never before?

1. "Five . . . Four . . . Three . . . Two . . . One . . . See ya!" and Chance McGuire, twenty-five, is airborne off a 600-foot concrete dam in Northern California. In one second he falls 15 feet, in two seconds 60 feet, and after three seconds and 130 feet, he is flying at 66 miles an hour. He prays that his parachute will open facing away from the dam, that his canopy won't collapse, that his goggles will be handy, and that no ill wind will slam him back into the cold concrete. The chute snaps open, the sound echoing through the gorge like a gunshot, and McGuire is soaring, carving S-turns into the air, swooping over a winding creek. When he lands, he is a speck on a path along the creek. He hurriedly packs his chute and then, clearly audible above the rushing water, lets out a war cry that rises past those people still sitting on the dam, past the commuters driving by on the roadway, past even the hawks who circle the ravine. It is a cry of defiance, thanks, and victory; he has survived another BASE jump.

2. McGuire is a practitioner of what he calls the king of all extreme sports. BASE—an acronym for building, antenna, span (bridge) and earth (cliffs)—jumping has one of the sporting world's highest fatality rates: in its 18-year history, forty-six participants have been killed. Yet the sport has never been more popular, with more than a thousand jumpers in the United States, and more seeking to get into it every day. It is an activity without margin for error. If your chute malfunctions, don't bother reaching for a reserve—there isn't time. There are no second chances.

3. Still, the sport may be a perfect fit with the times. As extreme a risk taker as McGuire seems, Americans may have more in common with him than they know or care to admit. America has embarked on a national orgy of thrill seeking and risk taking. The rise of adventure and extreme sports like BASE jumping, snowboarding, ice climbing, skateboarding, and paragliding is merely the most vivid manifestation of this new national bhavior.

4. The rising popularity of extreme sports speaks of an eagerness on the part of millions of Americans to participate in activities closer to the edge, where danger, skill, and fear combine to give weekend warriors and professional athletes alike a sense of pushing out personal boundaries. According to American Sports Data Inc., a consulting firm, participation in so-called extreme sports is way up. Snowboarding has grown 113 percent in five years and now boasts nearly 5.5 million participants. Mountain biking, skateboarding, scuba diving—the growth curves reveal a nation that loves to play with danger. Contrast that with activities like baseball, touch football, and aerobics, all of which were in steady decline throughout the 1990s.

5. The pursuits that are becoming more popular have one thing in common: the perception that they are somehow more challenging than a game of touch football. "Every human being with two legs, two arms is going to wonder how fast, how strong, how enduring he or she is," says Eric Perlman, a mountaineer and filmmaker specializing in extreme sports. "We are designed to experiment or die."

6. And to get hurt. More Americans than ever are injuring themselves while pushing their personal limits. In 1997, the U.S. Consumer Products Safety Commission reported that 48,000 Americans were admitted to hospital emergency rooms with skateboarding-related injuries. That's 33 percent more than the previous year. Snowboarding emergency room visits were up 31 percent; mountain climbing up 20 percent. By every statistical measure available, Americans are participating in and injuring themselves through adventure sports at an unprecedented rate.

7. Consider Mike Carr, an environmental engineer and paraglider pilot from Denver who last year survived a bad landing that smashed ten ribs and collapsed his lung. Paraglider pilots use feathery nylon wings to take off from mountain tops and float on thermal wind currents—a completely unpredictable ride. Carr also mountain bikes and climbs rock faces. He walked away from a 1,450 foot fall in Peru in 1988. After his recovery, he returned to paragliding. "This has taken over many of our lives," he explains. "You float like a bird out there. You can go as high as 17,000 feet and go for 200 miles. That's magic."

8. Previous generations did not need to seek out risk; it showed up uninvited and regularly: global wars, childbirth complications, diseases and pandemics from the flu to polio, dangerous products, and even the cold-war threat of mutually assured destruction. "I just don't think extreme sports would have been popular in a ground-war era," says Dan Cady, professor of popular culture at California State University at Fullerton. "Coming back from a war and getting onto a skateboard would not seem so extreme."

9. But for recent generations, many of those traditional risks have been reduced by science and government, leaving peo-

ple to face less real risk. Life expectancy has increased. Violent crime is down. Americans are 57 percent less likely to die of heart disease than their parents; smallpox, measles, and polio have virtually been eradicated in the United States.

10. War survivors speak of the terror and the excitement of being in a death match. "People are taking risks because everyday risk is minimized and people want to be challenged," says Joy Marr, forty-three, an adventure racer who was the only woman member of a five-person team that finished the 1998 Raid Gauloises, the granddaddy of all adventure races. This is a sport that requires several days of nonstop climbing, rafting and surviving through some of the roughest terrain in the world.

11. The question is, How much is enough? Without some expression of risk, people may never know their limits and therefore who they are as individuals. "If you don't assume a certain amount of risk," says paraglider pilot Wade Ellet, fifty-one, "you're missing a certain amount of life." And it is by taking risks that one may achieve greatness. "We create technologies, we make new discoveries, but in order to do that, we have to push beyond the set of rules that are governing us at that time," says psychologist Farley.

–Time Magazine

SCANNING FOR DETAILS

Answer these questions. Underline the details in the reading that support your answer.

1. How far does Chance McGuire jump and what is his maximum speed?

   _____

   _____

2. What does BASE stand for?

   _____

3. What other examples of extreme sports are there?

   _____

4. What has happened to:

   a. participation in snowboarding over the past five years?

      _____

   b. participation in baseball and touch football?

      _____

5. What does this change in popular sports tell us about Americans today?

   _____

6. What do the activities that are becoming popular have in common?

   _____

7. What injuries did Mike Carr get as a result of paragliding?

   _____

8. Why does he still do it?

   _____

9. Why did previous generations not have to look for risks?

   _____

10. Why is it important to have a certain amount of risk in life?

    _____

Work with a partner to ask and answer the questions. Look back at the reading if you cannot agree on the answers.

USING EVIDENCE TO SUPPORT IDEAS

It is very important to support ideas with examples, statistics, and explanations. For example, in paragraph 2 the author says: "BASE . . . jumping has one of the sporting world's highest fatality rates." This is followed by: "in its 18-year history, forty-six people have been killed."

Find other examples of this by going through the reading again and completing the following table. The first one has been done for you.

Idea	Support
1. Participation in extreme sports is way up.	Snowboarding has grown 113% in five years and now boasts nearly 5.5 million participants
2. More Americans are getting hurt.	a. _____ b. _____ c. _____ d. _____
3. _____ _____	The example of Mike Carr

Idea	Support
4. In the past, life was full of risk.	a. _____ b. _____ c. _____ d. _____ e. _____
5. _____ _____	a. Life expectancy increased b. Violent crime down c. _____ d. _____
6. _____	The example of Joy Marr

Check your answers with a partner. Refer to the article if necessary. Discuss why the evidence is convincing in each case.

After Reading

REACTING TO THE INFORMATION

The comments on the left were written in response to the article you just read. The statements on the right express different opinions. Read each comment quickly and match it with the opinion that summarizes it the best.

1. Taking part in risky activities makes us feel alive. It also satisfies our curiosity about our abilities—and how we handle challenge. It can completely focus your mind. There is nothing like it.

   a. _____ Risk takers are selfish.

2. Extreme sports are mostly solo activities that fail to teach us the valuable lessons of traditional sports—teamwork, cooperation, good sportsman-ship, and friendship. This is not social progress.

b. _____ Risk takers are bored.

3. Although taking part in risky activities may certainly be thrilling for the individual, the dangerous consequences affect the lives of not only the risk takers but also the families and partners. There is an underlying sense of selfishness to many forms of risks that know no limits.

c. _____ Risk taking makes us better people.

4. In today's world, millions of people live in fear every single single day of their lives, but there are a few who are so bored by their secure, middle-class existence that they jump off bridges to play with death. Why not put that desire for thrill into something meaningful like becoming a firefighter or a brain surgeon? Or if that kind of profession does not provide enough risk, why not volunteer for work in some war-filled country?

d. _____ Risk taking teaches us nothing.

Check your answers with a partner. Then discuss the following.

1. Which comments you agree with and why
2. Which comments you do not agree with and why
3. The general opinion on risk takers

State your own opinion in one or two sentences.

EVALUATING THE INFORMATION—REMOVING THE STEREOTYPING

To *stereotype* means to assume that certain people have certain characteristics. Very often that is not the case. So is it really true that people who participate in extreme activities do so only for the thrill and excitement? And is it really true that they are selfish, crazy, and fearless?

Paired Readings: Understanding Underlying Ideas

■ READING TIP: *The reader sometimes has to deduce what the writer is feeling or thinking. If the writer says, "The mountain is a mystical, majestic place," he means he really appreciates his surroundings.*

Climbing Mount Everest is still the most dangerous adventure known to mankind: for every four people who reach the peak, one dies in the effort. The following readings are personal accounts of two people who made it to the top. Choose one of the accounts and work with a partner who is reading the same one.

■■
_____

Reading 1: Jamie Clarke

Scanning/Highlighting: Read the article and highlight the sections that help us understand the following:

■ Jamie's appreciation of his surroundings
■ His reasons for climbing Mt. Everest
■ How he felt on the way
■ His actions on the summit

Jamie Clarke

1. The mountain environment is a mystical, majestic place. From the top of the tallest mountain in the world—the place the Sherpa people of Nepal call *Sagarmatha,* meaning "Forehead in the Sky"—the world below us curves away across the Tibetan Plateau to the north and across Nepal and Northern India to the south. Above, only a brilliant blue sky lies between us and the heavens.

2. This is a place among all places to comprehend the power of creation. It is a place that, above all, should elicit our respect and responsible behavior. Everest is not about dying. It is in every sense about being fully alive.

3. Men and women climb mountains for many reasons, most of them personal. For us, climbing Everest gave us the satisfaction of knowing we had accomplished the most difficult task most people could ever imagine. But personal success, even as we measure it by our climbing, is only meaningful when it leads us to better our performance in everything we do, to be different people today than we were yesterday, and to make a greater contribution to the world around us.

4. This was our third Everest expedition. In 1991 and again in 1994, we had gone to the mountain but failed to make the summit due to bad weather. After three years of preparation, we and the other members of our team arrived at Everest's southern base camp in early April 1997, determined to reach the top this time.

5. On May 5, we were ready to begin our summit push, when with a roar like an express train, jet-stream winds dropped onto the mountain and whipped plumes of snow off the upper slopes of Everest, killing five climbers on the north side. We waited for two weeks. By May 22, we were ready again. Seventy climbers from many countries were on the mountain that night. Suddenly the wind stopped. Under a crystal-clear full moon, we hurriedly ate and dressed. At 11.30 P.M., we stepped out onto the steep southeast shoulder of Mount Everest.

6. It was like going onstage. We had butterflies in our stomachs, and our minds wandered. Was our conditioning suited to the challenge? Would we be distracted by the state of other climbers? Would the winds try to blow us off the ridge?

7. I knew within the first hour that it was going to be a strong climb when I kept overtaking my Sherpa. I sensed that something extraordinary was happening. By the time we reached the Balcony, I was alone with two Sherpas.

8. I was transfixed by the rising sun on my right and the setting moon on my left. The immense shadow of Everest played across the clouds, and I imagined myself as a tiny dot trailing on the edge of the mountain. I felt it was a day for which I had been born. I was so filled with joy that I was giggling into my oxygen mask.

9. The most sobering moment in the climb came at the Hillary Step, a rock named for Sir Edmund Hillary that is less than 330 feet below the summit. In the middle of a tangle of ropes hung the body of Bruce Herrod, a South African who died on Everest in the spring of 1996. Pete Atans, an experienced American climber, had already discovered the body and was struggling to free it. I stopped to help. What might have been a simple task at sea level was treacherous and complicated on the rocks at this altitude, but we managed. In our own quiet ceremony, Pete and I committed the body to the mountain.

10. I then moved up onto the Summit Ridge. I can only describe it as a homecoming, even though I had never been there before. I felt I was standing on familiar ground. I knew this place and felt welcome.

11. Seven and a half hours after leaving the camp, Gyalbu and I joined the New Zealand team on the summit. I spent 45 minutes enjoying the view from the top of the world and taking the obligatory pictures. As the New Zealanders began to drift from the top, three of us remained gazing into the shadow-filled valleys from the only place that earthly shadows could not touch. Soon my Sherpa friends began their descent. I lingered utterly alone, standing with one foot in Nepal and the other in Tibet. I opened my arms, surrendered to the moment, turned 360 degrees, and saw the edges of the world dropping in all directions.

12. Although I was alone, I felt I was joined by my family, my friends, the people who shared our dream, and the thousands of schoolchildren around the world who had been following our expedition in their classrooms via the Internet. It was a shared achievement because I could not have done it by myself. It was a moment of complete happiness.

Practice talking about your article using only the highlighted information.

Reading 2: Alan Hobson

Scanning/Highlighting: Read the article and highlight the sections that help us understand the following:

- How afraid Alan felt and what he did about it
- His unwillingness to risk his life
- His actions on the summit
- Lessons learnt

Alan Hobson

1. As we started up the slope above the South Column, I was struck by how steep and hard the ice was. We were not using a fixed rope, and it became clear that the farther we moved from camp, the greater the danger became. As the angle of the slope increased, I focused on what would save my life, rather than on what might kill me.

2. By 1 A.M., I found myself mysteriously falling behind the rest of our group. Realizing that I might not be thinking clearly, I asked one of my Sherpas, Kami Tsering, to check my oxygen. I suddenly became cold and told him, "We have to go down—now!" But instead of turning around, he walked up to me and announced: "Nineteen ninety-one expedition—no summit. Nineteen ninety four—no summit. This expedition: very important summit."

3. Kami discovered I had been drawing on an empty oxygen bottle. He hooked up a new bottle for me, and I felt an immediate psychological and physical boost. I knew that if I could move, I could stay warm. So we trudged on, feeling confident, at least until the wind began gusting again at 2:30 A.M.

4. The wild blowing snow stole the moon, which had been lighting our way, and gave me a bad feeling about the mountain. Without warning, one of the gusts blasted me in the face and filled my hood with snow, which slipped down my back. At this point I wondered if I could continue, as I knew how quickly I would get cold up there.

5. As Kami and I came over the crest of the southeast ridge, a whole new world opened up. I could see the entire ridge and the South Summit. We had enough oxygen left for a decent shot at the top.

6. My other Sherpa, Tashi Tsering, was waiting on the Balcony—a shelf on the southeast ridge. "You need to let me know whether we can do it safely in the time allowed," I told him. "If we can't, we're going back down—right now." He turned to me and said, "No problem. Still early." I thought: "If the weather holds, we might just pull this off."

7. But we still had to cross the part that scared me the most—a knife-edged ridge with a 9,000-foot drop on the right into Tibet and a 5,000-foot drop on the left into Nepal.

8. Cranking my oxygen as far as it would go, I wanted to make sure that I was in control. Even so, my legs started shaking and I told myself: "This is just horrendous. Don't look down over the edge into the abyss, Alan." Passing an ice hole on the way, I stared down in disbelief—all the way down to the Kangshung Glacier, 9,000 feet below. "Just look at your feet, and follow the footsteps," I told myself.

9. I finally reached the summit, which is about 10 feet long and just wide enough to stand on. Tattered prayer flags and a discarded survey instrument littered the place. It was a bit of an eyesore, but it was also a sight for sore eyes.

10. Once there, I used my radio and announced: "Base camp: this is Hobson. I confirm arrival on the summit of Tashi Tsering, Kami Tsering, and myself at 9 A.M., May 23, 1997. Half the dream is done. If there is a lesson here, it's that if you hang on to your dreams long enough, you can achieve them." Then I started to cry with joy.

11. Within 15 minutes I had the pictures I needed to prove where I had been. But I had no desire to look at the view because I was still focused on not making any mistakes, on making my country proud—and on making it down alive. On Everest, it only counts if you make the round trip, and I didn't want anyone to be able to say, "I told you he couldn't do it."

12. On the way down I removed my mask because of an oxygen flow problem, suffering second-degree burns to my face as a result. I was so tired that my legs gave out and I fell—fortunately, I was clipped to a fixed rope at the time. I took some clexamethasone, a fast-acting anti-inflammatory, and things improved dramatically. By 2:30 in the afternoon, I was back at Camp IV. I was excited, satisfied, and exhausted.

13. We went to Everest with the personal goal of attaining the summit, but we also strove for a purpose higher than to simply stand on top of the world. Our adventure safely concluded, our goal will be to demonstrate how the lessons we learned on Everest can be applied to the world of business and the business of life. We want to do more than merely share a story about a couple of guys who climbed a mountain. In many ways, what we did was irrelevant. What is not irrelevant are the lessons we learned along the way: how to work as a team, how to overcome setbacks, how to deal with failure, how to push through pain and discomfort, and how to make dreams come true, whatever the obstacles. From Everest, we learned that it is unrealistic to expect to have success without failure. Failure is an integral part of success, because it is from failure that we learn.

Practice talking about your article using only the highlighted information.

RETELLING THE INFORMATION: MAKING A PROFILE

Work with somebody who read a different reading. Using your highlighting, take turns telling the stories of Jamie Clarke and Alan Hobson. Based on the information from both readings, make a profile (description) of people who participate in extreme activities like climbing Mt. Everest. Use the following outline to help you. Write the information in note form.

Reasons for climbing   _____

_____

_____

_____

Feelings during climb   _____

_____

_____

_____

Reaction to reaching the summit   _____

_____

_____

_____

How the experience will be used   _____

_____

_____

_____

_____

Use the information in the profile to support or destroy the various opinions on risk takers that were discussed on pages 58–59. Reevaluate your own opinion to see if it has changed.

Vocabulary Building

USING PUNCTUATION: COMMAS

Recognizing how punctuation is used can help us make sense of what we are reading. Commas are used to show a list of related terms, which can be nouns, adjectives, or actions in the form of single words or phrases.

Example: (From Paragraph 8 in the reading "Life On the Edge"): "Previous generations did not need to seek out risk; it showed up regularly: *global wars, childbirth complications, diseases and pandemics from the flu to polio, dangerous products,* and even the *cold war threat* of mutually assured destruction."

The commas indicate that there are five types of risks.

Complete the following exercise. All the examples are taken from the reading on pages 53–55.

1. (Paragraph 1) What four things does Chance McGuire pray for?

   _____   _____

   _____   _____

2. (Paragraph 1) What three actions is he doing?

   _____   _____

   _____

3. (Paragraph 1) What three feelings are expressed in his war cry?

_____   _____

_____

4. (Paragraph 3) Name five extreme sports mentioned in this paragraph.

_____   _____

_____   _____

_____

5. (Paragraph 4) What are the three characteristics of activities Americans are participating in?

_____   _____

_____

6. (Paragraph 4) In which three activities has participation declined?

_____   _____

_____

7. (Paragraph 9) What three diseases no longer exist in the United States?

_____   _____

_____

Check your answers with a partner.

Expanding Your Language

SPEAKING

A. Interviewing: Answer this questionnaire on risk taking. Check (✔) what is true or false for you.

	True	*False*
1. I do not like my opinions being challenged.	_____	_____
2. I would rather be an accountant than a TV anchor.	_____	_____
3. I believe that I control my destiny.	_____	_____
4. I am a highly creative person.	_____	_____
5. I do not like trying exotic foods.	_____	_____
6. Friends would call me a thrill seeker.	_____	_____
7. I like to challenge authority.	_____	_____
8. I prefer familiar things to new things.	_____	_____
9. I am known for my curiosity.	_____	_____
10. I would rather not travel abroad.	_____	_____
11. I am easily bored.	_____	_____
12. I have never gotten speeding tickets.	_____	_____
13. I am extremely adventurous.	_____	_____
14. I need a lot of stimulation in my life.	_____	_____
15. I would rather work for a salary than for a commission.	_____	_____
16. Making my own decisions is very important to me.	_____	_____

See Exercise page E–1 to evaluate yourself.

Interview three people who completed their questionnaires. Compare your information. Discuss the following:

- What did the questionnaire show about you?
- Do you agree with the result? Why? Why not? Give examples from your experience to support your answer.

Report on the similarities and differences in your group to others in the class.

B. Discussion: Using the information in this chapter and any information of your own, discuss the following:

- Is risk-taking behavior something we are born with, or does it depend on the way we are brought up?
- What are the advantages of risk-taking?
- If we feel that we are not taking enough risks, what can we do?

WRITING

A. Reaction Writing: Write your reaction to the following: (a) what you now think about risk takers; (b) whether or not you consider yourself a risk taker; (c) whether or not taking risks is in general a good idea.

B. Personal Writing: Think of a time when you were very nervous about doing something, but you still did it. Examples might be going on a journey or changing jobs. Think about why you were nervous, what made you do it anyway, how you felt afterwards. Make a short outline of your ideas in note form. Use your notes to write a one-page account of this incident.

CHAPTER 4

Taking a Break

 Chapter Openers

WHAT DO YOU THINK? TRUE OR FALSE

Think about the following statements. Circle *T* for true and *F* for false. Be ready to explain your answer.

1. T F   The concept of taking a vacation has existed only for the past 100 years.

2. T F   People take longer vacations now than in the past.

3. T F   People take more frequent vacations now than in the past.

4. T F   Advances in technology are making it hard for people to take time off.

5. T F   Taking a vacation requires a lot of time and money.

Compare your answers with a partner. Give reasons or examples to support what you say.

PERSONALIZING

Answer these questions for yourself. Compare what you wrote with two other students in the class.

1. What do you do on weekends or days off?
2. Given the choice, would you rather (a) watch TV or a video at home or (b) go out to a theater or concert?
3. Which of the following is the perfect length for a vacation? (a) less than 5 days; (b) 5–15 days; (c) 1 month; (d) more than 3 months.
4. Where do you like to go for your vacations?
5. What three activities do you do the most while on vacation?

Compare your answers with a partner or in a small group.

GETTING INFORMATION FROM A CHART

The following is a list of some activities that Americans like to do while on vacation. Rank them in terms of how popular you think each one is. Use *1* for most popular and *5* for least popular. Be prepared to support your choice. Compare your ranking with that of a partner.

Activity	Rank
Gambling	
National/state park	
Golfing/tennis/skiing	
Museum	
Theme/amusement park	
Shopping	
Beach	

Check your ranking against the chart on Exercise page E–1. How accurate were you? Which activity is actually the most popular? The least popular? Why do you think that is the case?

Exploring and Understanding Reading

PREVIEWING

The following reading is about how the concept of vacations developed. Read only the title and the subtitle, then predict three ideas that will be discussed.

1. _____

2. _____

3. _____

SKIMMING

Skim the reading and see if your predictions were correct. If you think you were wrong, change your prediction. After your quick reading, check the statement that most accurately reflects the information in the reading.

Paid vacations began when

1. _____   people started having more time.

2. _____   there was a change in work style.

3. _____   people started having more money.

The Rise and Fall of Vacations

By Felicia R. Lee

The vacation is a relatively new concept and an evolving one, with the line between work and play now becoming blurred by communications technology.

1. Once upon a time the rich played when the mood struck and almost everybody else worked on their farms all week and relaxed for one day at the end of the week. Although August is now established as top vacation time, few people realize that their paid vacation is a fairly recent phenomenon. The word "vacation" was not even in the dictionary until the middle of the nineteenth century.

2. According to historians, vacation is a reflection of what is happening in society in terms of work and resources available. "You can't have vacations without a certain kind of class with the resources and the time to take vacations," said Cindy S. Aron, an associate professor of history at the University of Virginia. "That does not really happen until the first half of the twentieth century.

3. The popular vacation owes its birth to such factors as the changing nature of work and the rise of the railroad. In the nineteenth century, most people in North America were farmers, artisans, or self-employed in some way. Wealthy people went off to play while others went away primarily for their health. But as the industrial revolution took place, North America was transformed from an agricultural into an urban-industrial society, and by the end of the century more men were working for a salary in the growing corporate world. Working for industry meant working by the clock. People started separating work from life. They started thinking in terms of "after work" and weekends and retirement. Vacation places therefore started to take shape as there developed a new middle class that had money in its pockets, some free time, and a taste for amusement.

4. Interestingly enough, however, this division between work and life is now becoming blurred again. The technological revolution that we are living in at the present has brought with it cellular telephones, fax machines, e-mail, and the Internet. This has made people much more available. Combine this with the American anxiety to work harder in order to do more, buy more, and be better, and what happens very often is that people continue to work even while on vacation. Indeed, the trend now seems to be that although North Americans are getting more paid leave then they did 10 years ago, they are taking shorter but more frequent vacations. And sure enough, the computer and the cellular phone go along too.

–The New York Times

NOTE TAKING: UNDERSTANDING REASONS

The article discusses the development of vacations using three different time periods. Complete the following outline to show the development as well as the reasons for it.

Main Points (time period)	Details (reasons)
A. Before industrial revolution	1. *Only rich had money & time*
	2. *No real vacation*
B. During and after industrial revolution	1. _____
	2. _____
	3. *People ruled by the clock*
C. Technological revolution	1. _____
	2. _____
	3. _____

Step 1. Compare your notes with a partner. If you do not have the same or similar ideas in your outline, check the information in the reading.

Step 2. Use your notes to explain the information. Take turns talking about each stage.

APPLYING THE INFORMATION

Discuss the following questions using both the information you just read and your own personal experience.

1. Are people indeed taking shorter, more frequent vacations?

2. What kind of break would somebody who works hard prefer?

■ One that has scheduled activities

■ One that has no schedule

PAIRED READINGS

The following readings are about two different vacation styles. Work with a partner who is reading the *same* one.

■■

Reading 1: Getting Down in the Dirt

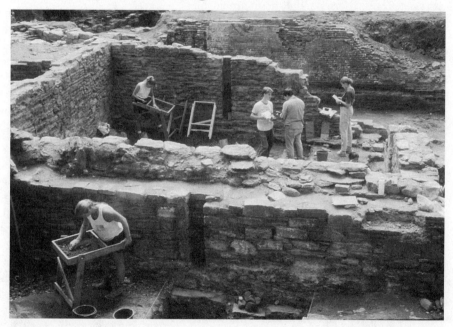

SKIMMING

Read the article quickly and then answer the following questions.

1. What kind of activities do people participate in on these trips?

_____

2. What are the characteristics of people who go on these trips?

_____

Getting Down in the Dirt

By Felicity Dunn

Amateur archaeologists spend their holidays digging up the distant past.

1. The wake-up knock on the door comes at 5:45 A.M. By 6 A.M. you've had a snack, walked to the site and are digging in the dirt. At 9 A.M. there's a half-hour break for breakfast. Then it's back to work. After lunch—and a siesta—there are lectures or field trips. Dinner's at 7 P.M. and suggested bedtime is 9 P.M.

2. Some people might think this is an odd way to spend a vacation, but not archaeologist Mina Cohn, who came to Canada from her native Israel in 1980. "Working on digs myself, I met people who were not professionals, who came and joined our excavations and I saw how much they enjoyed it," the Ottawa resident said in an interview. "When I came to Canada I heard many people say they would like to join an excavation but did not know how. And some people said to me, 'Why don't you do it because you have the experience?'" So she went back to school to study business, allied herself with an Ottawa travel agency and launched Archaeological Encounters, a travel company offering trips to Israel.

3. What makes Cohn's trips different is that they combine time on a dig with a traditional guided tour of the country. On a two-week trip, participants spend five or six days working on a dig while staying at a nearby kibbutz, and the remainder touring Israel in the comfort of a coach, staying at first class hotels.

4. Each trip has a core group consisting of an archaeology professor and students from the University of Ottawa. But anybody interested in history, archaeology or culture—and in a different vacation—can join the expeditions. "As long as the person is in good health and they could work in their own garden, they could join the dig," Cohn says.

5. The digs are centered on an excavation site south of the Sea of Galilee that dates from about 3,000 B.C., making it one of the oldest settlements in the Middle East. Major work at the 150-hectare site began in 1986. Among the things that have been unearthed are a colonnaded Roman street, an amphitheater, and a bath house. Hundreds of scientists and laborers work there year round. "It's a fascinating place that keeps surprising everybody every day," says Cohn.

6. Twelve-day trips from Ottawa or Montreal to Israel cost approximately $2,500 per person. This includes everything except taxes, insurance, and tips for the guide and the bus driver. There is a minimum of fifteen people and a maximum of forty on the tours. At the dig, participants are divided into smaller groups and work under the on-site archaeologists. "We dig," says Cohn. "We do exactly what archaeologists do. We work with the area supervisor and we progress and by the end of the week we have an understanding of what digging is."

7. She is thinking of offering vacations elsewhere and has made contact with archaeologists in Greece, Italy, and Mexico.

–The Canadian Press

SCANNING FOR DETAILS

Look back at the reading for the answers to these questions. Mark the question number in the margin of the page. Write your answers in note form.

1. What is the typical daily schedule?

   5:45 A.M. _____

   _____   _____

   _____   _____

   _____   _____

   _____   _____

   _____   _____

   9 P.M. _____

2. What two things did Mina Cohn have to do in order to start her company?

   _____

   _____

3. What kind of people would be interested in this kind of a trip?

   _____

   _____

4. What requirements must they meet?

_____

_____

5. How big and how old is the site?

_____

_____

6. What is not included in the cost?

_____

7. Where else might the trips go?

_____

Check your answers with a partner. Refer to the reading if you do not agree.

NOTE TAKING: GROUPING SIMILAR INFORMATION

Scan the reading quickly and complete the outline using the following steps:

- Find the information corresponding to each main idea
- Highlight the key words and/or phrases
- Use the highlighted information to make notes

■ READING TIP:
When making notes, it is not always necessary to follow the order of the information as it is presented in the reading. It is better to group the details that deal with the same idea together.

■ TIP: *To make things easier, you can use a different colored highlighter for each main idea.*

Main Points	**Details**
A. Introduction	*interesting vacation*
	different from normal
	archeological dig
B. Origin of idea	
Who	_____
From	_____
How started	_____

Main Points	**Details**
C. Trip	
Overall schedule	_____
	_____
Daily schedule	_____
	_____
	_____
	_____
	_____
	_____
	_____
D. Excavation site	
Where	_____
How old	_____
Size	_____
Findings	_____
E. Participants	_____
Number	_____
Background	_____
Requirements	_____
F. Cost	
	_____
	_____
G. Future plans	_____

RECAPPING THE INFORMATION

Work with a partner who took notes about the same story. Take turns explaining the information to each other. As you talk, make sure that you mention each main idea first and then discuss it. (See Note, page 74).

■ ■

Reading 2: A Day at the Spa

SKIMMING

Read the article quickly and answer the following questions.

1. What are the different services that are offered at spas?

   _____

2. What are the characteristics of people who go to spas?

   _____

A Day at the Spa

By Tamala M. Edwards

For the stressed out, the time pressed and the bone weary, indulgence is just around the corner.

1. Avon, the cosmetics company, knew it was time for a change. To present a new face, it opened a day spa on New York City's Fifth Avenue: a 20,000-square-foot pleasure palace painted in cool shades of celery and dove and full of overstuffed furniture and antiques. Top stylists snip and color hair, usually after guests have had massages, facials, mud packs, or nail services. "With career and mothering, I don't have time," says TV producer Colleen Crowe, 39. But every few weeks, she'll break away for a leisurely manicure, haircut, and massage. "Just walking down the hall feels luxurious."

2. These days, when the wallets are fat and time is slim, the day spa is the thing. Demand for quick treats has driven up the number of such spas from 30 in 1989 to 1,600 in 1999, according to *Spa Finders* magazine. Not all of them are full-service emporiums like Avon. Hairdressers are rubbing backs, department stores are doing aromatherapy, and gyms are packing mud. There are spa-mobiles that bring the services to your home, and special teen packages for your kids. Some even offer home cleaning services while you spoil yourself. "The business is going nuts," says Peggy Wynne Borgman, a Saratoga, California, spa owner and consultant.

3. Traditionally, spas were places for the sick to benefit from the minerals in hot springs; later they were known mainly as fat farms. Spas got a better reputation as luxurious destinations like Canyon Ranch and Golden Door opened in the 1960s and 1970s, but these paradises were seen as remote retreats for the rich and famous. In the 1990s, day spas have attracted a more diverse crowd, people who can't afford to spend thousands and linger for a week. "I can't get away for that long," says Connecticut motivational speaker Ronni Burns, 47, who gets a massage and facial twice a month. "I find that much relaxing stressful." One-third of spa goers make $45,000 or less a year. Half are between ages thirty-four and fifty-two. And it is not only women that take advantage of these places. A quarter of spa goers are men.

4. Indeed, day spas have evolved from an indulgence to an expected "extra." Joan Haratani, an attorney who soaks in a whirlpool and gets a massage once a week at Oakland's Claremont Hotel, explains, "I don't consider it a luxury. It's an absolute necessity." Some health insurance providers, such as Blue Cross of California, now cover at least some spa treatments if prescribed by a physician, and companies like Hewlett-Packard are hiring on-site massage therapists for their employees.

5. The fanciest day spas have become quite an experience. Thick robes, mineral water and wine, gourmet buffets, fresh flowers, and piped-in music are typical features. In Las Vegas, Canyon Ranch has opened a 16,000-square-foot day spa—the largest in the country—at the Venetian Resort-Hotel-Casino. Customers there can soak and get an underwater massage in a private pool filled with flowers. For the best experience, visitors will soon be able to steam and cover themselves in mud in a room where fiber-optic cable replicates the night sky. A soft rain from the fake night dome washes them clean.

6. One problem is that the quality of day spas can vary widely. Many cannot live up to their extravagant advertisements that promise renewed energy and eternal youth. Yet they may do some good. A survey at the University of Miami found that twenty-six adults given 15-minute back rubs twice a week for 5 weeks showed signs of less stress, were less depressed, and performed better on math tests. Something must be working.

–Time Magazine

SCANNING FOR DETAILS

Look back at the reading for the answers to these questions. Mark the question number in the margin of the page. Write your answers in note form.

1. Why doesn't Colleen Crowe have time?

   _____

2. How many spas were there in 1989? 1999?

   _____

3. Why are day spas becoming so popular?

   _____

4. How can you get part of your treatment paid for?

   _____

5. Where is the largest spa in the country?

   _____

6. What is one problem with spas?

_____

7. What did the survey at the University of Miami show?

_____

Check your answers with a partner. Refer to the reading if you do not agree.

NOTE TAKING: GROUPING SIMILAR INFORMATION

See the Reading Tip on page 78.

Scan the reading quickly and complete the outline following these steps:

- Find the information corresponding to each main idea.
- Highlight the key words and/or phrases.
- Use the highlighted information to make notes.

Main Idea	Details
A. Introduction	*day spa becoming popular*
	30 in 1989 — 1,600 in 1999
B. Why popular	
Colleen Crowe	_____
	_____
Ronni Burns	_____
	_____
Joan Haratani	_____
	_____

■ **READING TIP:** *To make things easier, you can use a different colored highlighter for each main idea.*

Main Idea	Details
C. Description/services	
Expensive	
Avon	
Where	_____
Size	_____
Colors	_____
Services	_____
	_____
Venetian Resort	
Where	_____
Size	_____
Pool	_____
Special room	_____
Other	
Department stores	_____
Gyms	_____
Spa mobiles	_____
Home	_____
Companies	_____
D. Type of clients	
Sex	_____
Salary	_____
Age	_____
E. Problems/benefits	
Quality	_____
	_____

Main Idea	Details
Study	_____
	_____

RECAPPING THE INFORMATION

Work with a partner who took notes about the same reading. Take turns explaining the information to each other. As you talk, make sure that you mention each main idea first and then discuss it. (See Note, page 74).

After Reading

RETELLING THE INFORMATION

Work with a partner who took notes about the other reading. Use your notes to talk about the reading. Make sure you say what the main ideas are before you give the details.

REACTING TO THE INFORMATION: COMPARE AND CONTRAST

Discuss these questions based on the information from both readings as well as on any information of your own.

1. In what way do these readings show that the way we are taking vacations is changing?
2. What are the similarities and differences in terms of clients? In terms of activities?
3. Assuming that the overall cost is the same, would it be better to (a) go on a two-week vacation once a year, or (b) spend one day a month at a day spa? Think about the benefits you would get in each case.

APPLYING THE INFORMATION: EXPLORING THE BENEFITS

What can we get from a vacation other than a rest and a break from work (or school)?

SKIMMING

The following article is about adventure travel. Read through the article quickly and list four things that can happen as a result of going on an adventure vacation.

_____

_____

_____

_____

Wild at Heart

By Sammantha Dunn

1. The horse ran away with her once, she was scared on several occasions, and she thought about quitting at least ten times in the first day alone. For Jane Wolfberg, this was nothing like her quiet life as a legal secretary in Los Angeles, where the most excitement she faced was the occasional traffic jam.

2. Wolfberg made it through that first day, and the second. And then it happened. She gave the command and the horse cantered on cue. It felt like lifting off. Then there was the drumming of hooves underneath her. More than that, it was as if Scotland itself opened up; she saw shades of green previously unknown to her, marveled at the beauty of the pinkish-purple blooms, and the stinging sea breeze took her breath away. There were moments while covering the steep, hilly terrain that she thought, "I hope my horse doesn't trip and fall on me."

The shared thrill brought her close to her fellow riders on the trip. They all rode until the sun finally set, at 11 P.M. "It was exhilarating and scary, but I felt really alive. I realized then there's a part of me that had been craving this," recalls Wolfberg. "On these trips all my senses are completely in the moment. There are very few things I do in the rest of my life that are like that."

3. But she wants them to be. Her first step after Scotland was to join a hunt club at home. She now rides regularly. "Things that used to scare me don't scare me so much anymore, but I have yet to translate that into all aspects of my life. I would like to be more risk taking, not just physically but socially, be more outspoken and ask for things I want," she says. "These trips are about peak experience, but I want to have peak experiences here, where I live. I am looking for ways to bring that into my everyday life, to have peak experiences during the other 50 weeks of the year."

throw off old definitions of ourselves and try on a new definition."

Women and Wanderlust

4. Wolfberg is not alone in her search for where the wild things are. Sixty-three percent of adventure travelers are women, according to Marybeth Bond, a Northern California-based online travel columnist at www.ivillage.com and author of numerous travel books.

5. What is the reason for this? Bond says that it is the result of the swinging of the pendulum away from "historic confinements." A woman was almost always under the protection of a man when she traveled, if she was allowed to travel at all. The heiress who could pay for herself was rare. "With the shift of economic power in the West, and with more women traveling for business, the natural extension is for women to travel for pure discovery and adventure," Bond explains.

6. As well, a growing body of travel literature, movies, and documentaries provides images of female adventurers, meaning we have more role models than previous generations dared dream of. "When you hear inspiring and remarkable tales, it makes you think, 'If she had the guts to get up and go, maybe I can,'" says Bond, who herself is a perfect example. At age thirty, tired of the confines of corporate life, Bond gave up a great job in marketing to travel around the world by herself for two years. She trekked the Himalayas, lived with Hmong villagers in Vietnam, even rode camels across the Sahara and elephants in Asian jungles. "Travel," she says, "is a powerful way to

Inward Bound

7. In fact, adventure travel rarely seems to be a random choice among vacationers. Very often it coincides with a special event—a divorce, a birthday, a promotion, or an anniversary. "I think many people go on these trips with a hope or expectation or inner desire to find a different path in life. I know I have done that," says Richard Bangs, cofounder of Mountain Travel/Sobek in El Cerrito, Washington, which for 30-plus years has offered safaris, sea kayaking, trekking, hiking, photo expeditions, biking, camel treks, and wildlife tours worldwide for all skill levels.

8. Bangs speaks this from personal experience: "I have been in circumstances in my life where I did not like what was happening around me. So I said, 'It's time for a trip!' Not only do you get a new and better perspective, you also come back empowered to make a change."

First Day of the Rest of Your Life

9. Indeed, adventure is always life altering—whether or not you plan it being that way. Melanie Stern, a health care professional in Washington, D.C., says that when she took her first biking trip in 1987, she had no idea it would become such a passion that by the year 2000 she would have completed seventeen trips. "Biking has given me a confidence I never had before," says Stern.

"I have done 100-mile vacation trips, and after you do that you just feel incredible about yourself. When I was growing up, I was the kind of person who dropped classes and got bored. Now I know that while it may take me longer, I will get through anything. I will persevere."

10. Even more than that, Stern developed relationships with fellow travelers that have spanned almost a decade. "Now I know people across the country, and we go on a lot of trips together."

11. Stern's experience, says Bangs, is not an exception, "These trips are great places for relationships to develop," he says. "What you wear, what kind of car you drive, those things are meaningless. A person's inner personality is what is important and you get to know that very quickly. You see each other at your best and at your worst, you laugh together and experience excitement together."

—Shape

USING QUOTES

Read the article again and find the following quotes or parts of quotes. Identify the speaker and note the particular benefit that person was able to get. Discuss how each person's experience led to that particular benefit.

1. "Things that used to scare me don't scare me so much anymore . . . . I would like to be more risk taking, not just physically but socially, be more outspoken and ask for things I want."

   _____

2. "Travel is a powerful way to throw off old definitions of ourselves and try on a new definition."

   _____

3. "Not only do you get a new and better perspective, you also come back empowered to make a change."

   _____

4. "Now I know that while it may take me longer, I will get through anything. I will persevere."

   _____

Vocabulary Building

COLORS

In English, and probably in many other languages, names of colors are based on things like fruits, vegetables, animals, and so on.

Example: ". . . a 20,000-square-foot palace painted in cool shades of *celery* and *dove*." *Celery* is a vegetable and in this case refers to *light green*. *Dove* is a bird and refers to *pale gray*.

The following list of terms names five different colors. Fill in the color each term refers to.

TERM	COLOR
Peach	_____
Petroleum	_____
Cream	_____
Brick	_____
Mint	_____

Check your answers with a partner.

Think of at least ten more terms.

Check your list with the teacher.

Pair up with a classmate and take turns testing each other on the terms you listed.

PARALLELISM

The following sentences are taken from the reading "Getting Down in the Dirt."

- *So she <u>went</u> back to school to study business, <u>allied</u> herself with an Ottawa travel agency and <u>launched</u> Archeological Encounters...*
- *This includes everything except for <u>taxes</u>, <u>insurance</u>, and <u>tips</u> for the guide and bus driver.*

The underlined words make up a list and they all have the same form. The first sentence contains a list of the things that Mina Cohn had to do, and they are all in the simple past tense. The second sentence lists what the cost includes. In this case, the words are all in noun form. This is called *parallelism*. It is incorrect to have a sentence in which the different things that are listed are not in the same form.

Example: *I like to swim, play tennis, and mountain climbing.*

The preceding sentence should read: *I like swimming, playing tennis, and climbing mountains.* Or *I like to swim, play tennis and mountain climb.*

A. Scan the readings in this chapter and find five other examples of parallelism.

1. _____

_____

2. _____

_____

3. _____

_____

4. _____

_____

5. _____

_____

Check your examples with a partner. Check with your teacher if you are not sure.

B. Find the mistakes in the following sentences and then try to correct them.

1. The advantages of not drinking are to save money, think more clearly, drive more safely on the road, and healthy.

_____

_____

2. Alcohol affects people physically, psychologically, and their social relations with their families.

_____

_____

3. This shampoo makes your hair look more healthy, less chance of falling out, and grow faster.

_____

_____

4. Cellular phones have reduced our vacation time, are frustrating our families, and increased our stress.

_____

_____

Check your answers with a partner and ask your teacher if you are not sure.

Expanding Your Language

SPEAKING

Two-Minute Talk: Think of a vacation that you had as a child and a vacation that you had recently. Prepare some notes based on the following list.

- A description of each vacation
- What you liked/did not like about each vacation
- Any similarities or differences between the two

Practice speaking from your notes a few times. Present your information to a partner or make a tape for your teacher.

The Perfect Vacation: Several years ago (in the 1980s), Japanese companies were trying to encourage their employees to take more time off. They set up a competition, "Dream Vacation." The person who could think of the most interesting , exotic vacation would win. The prize was that he or she would go on this vacation with all expenses paid.

Try the same idea as follows:

1. Work with a partner or in a small group. Using your own imagination or material from a tourist agency (or the Internet), plan a two-week vacation.
2. Make a 5-minute presentation to the class about your trip.
3. After all the presentations have been made, discuss each one in your small groups and choose the one you like the most.

WRITING

Reaction Writing: Do you agree with the ideas presented in this chapter?

Example: Do you agree that technology is affecting us negatively in terms of vacation? Would you take any of the vacations described?

Topic Writing: Write about the following topic or a related topic of your own.

1. Why is it important to take a vacation?

Follow these steps to prepare your writing.

1. Think of three important reasons for vacations.
2. Outline four or five details for each reason.
3. Write about each reason in a separate paragraph.

Read On: Taking it Further

Ask your teacher to recommend some real-life adventure books for you to choose from. Reading these stories is a good way of finding out more about why people take certain risks.

Suggestions: *Into Thin Air* is the story of one fatal expedition to Mount Everest. *Into the Wild* is the story of a young man who gives away most of what he owns and goes into the wilderness of Alaska. *The Reader's Digest*, which is a monthly magazine, also has one real-life adventure in every issue. You can find it in your local library or on newspaper stands.

3

Time Matters

To everything there is a season . . . and a time to every purpose under heaven.

– Eccles. 3:1–10

93

Introducing the Topics

Time is not just an idea, but is an ever-present reality in our lives. In this unit you will read about time in the twenty-first century. Is our experience of time the same as it used to be? Chapter 5 looks at what some writers have to say about our fast-paced world and how speed is influencing our lives. Chapter 6 probes the topic of procrastination and its effect on our lives. You'll look at the issue of time management and how to cope with the demands on our time and energy in a positive way.

Points of Interest

OUR EXPERIENCE OF TIME

Do we have control over our time (active), or is time out of our control (passive)? Check (✔) the category you think fits each of these expressions. Write what you think each expression means. The first one has been done for you.

Expression	Active	Passive
1. If you want something done, ask a busy person. *Busy people know how to use their time well.*	✔	
2. Time waits for no one.		
3. A stitch in time saves nine.		
4. Time is money, look to the clock.		

Expression	Active	Passive
5. Time heals all wounds.		
6. A watched pot never boils.		
7. Never put off until tomorrow, the things you can do today.		
8. You can't hurry love.		
9. Work expands to fill the time available.		

Work with a partner or a small group. Compare the categories you chose, and explain what the expression means to you. Discuss the following questions.

- Is today's world too fast paced or not?
- Do we have more control over time today than in the past?

CHAPTER 5

Are We in a Race Against Time?

Chapter Openers

WHAT'S YOUR OPINION? AGREE OR DISAGREE

Circle *A* if you agree or *D* if you disagree with the statement.

1. A   D   Most days I have enough time to do the things I plan to do.

2. A   D   Thanks to technology like computers and cell phones, it takes less time to get work done than it used to.

3. A   D   I often feel that I don't have enough time to spend with friends and family.

4. A   D   In the future, I expect to have more time to do the things I want to do.

Work with a partner or a small group. Compare your ideas. Explain your ideas using reasons and examples.

PAIRED READINGS

Matching Meanings

Match each phrase in Column A with the explanation that best fits from Column B.

Column A

_____ 1. addicted to speed

_____ 2. multitasking

_____ 3. status symbol

_____ 4. sound bite

_____ 5. totally wired

_____ 6. on a high

Column B

a. doing more than one or two things at a time

b. something that shows a high position in society

c. a short piece of information that can be played on television or radio

d. unable or unwilling to slow down

e. feeling a rush of energy

f. electronically connected to the world

Work with a partner to check your answers.

The readings that follow present different points of view about how we experience time today. Choose one of the readings. Work with a partner who is reading the same information.

■ ■
_____

Reading 1: Living in the Accelerated Lane and Loving It. The Argument for Speed

SKIMMING

Read the article quickly and answer the following question: Do we like to live our lives in the fast lane? Why or why not?

_____

SCANNING

Scan the article for the answers to the following questions. Underline the words in the article that support the answer.

1. Who is James Gleick, and what has he done?

   _____

2. According to Gleick, how do we feel about the effect of speed on our lives?

   _____

3. What happens when we're multitasking (doing more than one thing at a time)?

   _____

4. How do many people feel about being too busy?

   _____

5. According to John Robinson, why do people lead rushed lives?

   _____

USA TODAY

Living in the accelerated lane and loving it

The argument in favor . . .

By Kim Painter

We might as well admit it: We're addicted to speed.

We like our fast computers, fast food, fast news, quick-cut videos and instant best sellers. We are channel-clicking, speed-dialing, Web-surfing, FedEx-sending, pager-checking, finger-tapping speedaholics.

It isn't all good for us; it certainly comes with a cost.

But please don't take our e-mail away.

That's the world according to James Gleick (rhymes with click), author of the new book *Faster: The Acceleration of Just About Everything* (Pantheon Books, $24).

Those who fear that all this speed is killing us — or at least deadening our souls — are missing a crucial point, Gleick says.

We love the rush.

"We know that when we're multitasking, we don't do any one task as well as we'd like. We know that fast food is just a synonym for mediocre food," he says. "And yet, that's us, standing in line at McDonald's and Burger King. Nobody is holding a gun to our heads," Gleick argues.

"We know we're giving up time to read great novels or listen to symphonies when we spend hours playing computer games, chatting on line or clicking through the TV channels.

"We tell ourselves that we're too busy to do X, but what we really mean is that we'd rather do Y."

And we are busy, he says — though maybe not as busy as we like to think.

"One of the sillier things we're going through now is that it's become a status symbol to be busy," he says. "People boast about being too busy to have lunch; they boast about being the first one at the office."

"We're all perpetrators and we're all victims," he says. "We can't stop ourselves from going to the beach with a cell phone tucked in our bathing suits."

John Robinson, a sociologist at the University of Maryland who specializes in time-use studies, says Gleick has it right: People leading the most-rushed lives have largely chosen them.

"There's a high involved in living this way," he says. "These multitaskers are trying to see just how far they can push it."

Compare your answers with a partner. Try to agree on the same answer. Look back at the reading if you disagree.

RECAPPING THE INFORMATION: HIGHLIGHTING

> ■ **READING TIP:**
> *Remember that high-lighting is a useful strategy for **finding** and **remembering** **facts** and **ideas** you read.*

A. Highlight the information that shows how attracted we are to living a fast-paced life.

B. Compare the information you highlighted to that of a partner. Add or note corrections to your highlighting. Using the high-lighted information, explain the important evidence about today's fast-paced life.

C. Together, list in note form evidence that shows some people like a fast-paced life.

REACTING TO THE INFORMATION

Discuss these questions with a partner or in a small group. Explain the reasons for your answers.

- What are some of the attractions of a fast-paced life?
- How does the acceleration of the information age affect our lives?
- Can the pace of life become too fast? How do we feel when that happens?
- Do you agree with the following statements taken from the reading?
  a. "We love the rush."
  b. "We stand in line at Burger King. Nobody is holding a gun to our heads."
  c. "We're all perpetrators and we're all victims."
  d. "There's a high involved in living this way."

■ ■
_____

Reading 2: Living in the Accelerated Lane and Loving It. The Argument Against Speed

SKIMMING

Read the information and answer the following questions.

Do we like to live our lives in the fast lane? Why or why not?

_____

USA TODAY

Living in the accelerated lane and loving it?

The argument against . . .

By Kim Painter

James Gleick, a respected science author and former *New York Times* columnist, has written the book on speed, a quick-paced compendium on everything from the history of watches to the evolution of the sound bite.

The story of how we reached this quickened pace "is not just a story, but the story of our time," he says.

But not everyone will recognize himself or herself in Gleick's technoworld.

Gerald Celente, director of the Trends Research Institute in Rhinebeck, N.Y., says Gleick is talking about a particular species, "thirty-somethings who brag about working 65–70 hour weeks . . . people who are totally wired all the time."

But there are people who still don't own a cell phone, much less take it to the beach. Celente is one of them: "I don't feel that if someone is out of contact with me for an hour, it's going to have serious consequences.

"There's a danger in making the extreme appear to be the norm . . . Why should this wired maniac be held up as the standard for everyone else?"

Gleick is aware that a few people still don't have personal computers and have never received an instant message. But the change in the culture is pervasive, he says, and touches everyone. After all, there's hardly a town in America that doesn't have CNN and MTV, microwave ovens and Egg McMuffins.

And he recognizes that something — a lot even — has been lost with all this speed and convenience.

"Pauses are an essential part of human life, and we are squeezing them out," he says. "The Sabbath was a pause, a crucial pause, for many humans . . . There was until recently a pause in stock trading at the end of the day. Now the world markets go all the time. There used to be a natural pause in the news cycle between the evening newspapers and the morning news. Now that is gone."

Gleick speculates that the culture may be nearing "a speed limit," running up against "the limit of how much information we can process in a day or how much information we can process in 30 seconds."

SCANNING

Look at the reading for the answers to the following questions. Underline the words in the reading that support the answer.

1. Who is James Gleick, and what has he done?

   _____

2. According to Gerald Celente, who are the people that Gleick is describing?

   _____

3. How does Celente feel about the need for a cell phone? Why?

   _____

4. According to Gleick, who is affected by the conveniences of a fast-paced life?

   _____

5. What are three examples of the pauses that have been lost in today's world?

   a. _____

   b. _____

   c. _____

Compare your answers with a partner. Try to agree on the same answers. Look back at the reading if you disagree.

RECAPPING THE INFORMATION: HIGHLIGHTING

A. Highlight the information that shows the dangers and dissatisfactions of living a fast-paced life.

■ *READING TIP:* Look at the information on page 101 for tips on highlighting.

B. Compare the information you highlighted to that of a partner. Add or note corrections to your highlighting. Using the highlighted information, explain the important criticisms about today's fast-paced life that are made in this reading selection.

C. Together, make a list of the evidence that shows there is criticism of our fast-paced life.

REACTING TO THE INFORMATION

Discuss these questions with a partner or in a small group. Explain the reasons for your answers.

- What are some examples that show evidence of our fast-paced life?
- How do we feel when the pace of life becomes too fast?
- What are some things that we can do to slow down?
- Do you agree with the following statements found in the reading?
  a. "I don't feel that if someone is out of contact with me for an hour, it's going to have serious consequences."
  b. "Pauses are an essential part of our human life and we are squeezing them out."
  c. "There is a limit of how much information we can process in a day . . . ."

After Reading

RETELLING THE INFORMATION

Work with a partner who read different information. Use the highlighted information and the list of evidence you made. Explain the ideas expressed in the reading. Choose two of the questions from the "Reacting to the Information" sections to discuss.

REACTING TO THE READING

Based on the information from both readings, complete the fol-

lowing chart that shows a comparison of two different approaches to life.

Characteristics of a fast-paced life	Characteristics of a slower-paced life
1. *fast food such as Egg McMuffins*	*pauses such as Sabbath*
2.	
3.	

Based on your comparison and ideas of your own, discuss the following question: Which do you prefer, life in the fast lane or life in the slow lane? Be prepared to give reasons for your choice.

Exploring and Understanding Reading

In the reading that follows, the writer offers some thoughts and opinions about the North American experience of waiting.

PRE-READING QUESTIONS

Discuss these questions with a partner or in a small group. Explain the reasons for your answers.

- List four examples of times in your daily routine when you might have to wait.

  Waiting in line at the cafeteria

  _____

  _____

  _____

- How does waiting make you feel? Explain the reasons why.
- Is waiting more difficult in North America than in other places? Why or why not?
- Do rich people end up having to wait less than the poor do? Explain your opinion.

MATCHING MEANINGS

Match each word or expression in Column A with the definition that best fits it in Column B.

Column A

_____ 1. bland

_____ 2. curse

_____ 3. contemplate

_____ 4. put down

_____ 5. hibernating

_____ 6. punctual

Column B

a. make fun of someone

b. on time

c. inactive or in a state of sleep

d. use bad language

e. ordinary

f. think about something over a
   period of time

Work with a partner to check your answers.

SKIMMING

READING TIP: *As you read, remember to concentrate on those ideas that you understand and continue to read through the entire essay before re-reading.*

Read the complete essay quickly and answer this question: *According to the writer, is the experience of waiting positive, negative, or both? Be prepared to give examples to support your answer.*

_____

_____

THE GAZETTE, MONTREAL

I could just scream

By Peter Carlson, *Washington Post*

WASHINGTON—The music is driving you nuts. It's so cheerful, it's depressing. It's so bland, it's offensive. Suddenly it stops, and you get excited: could this be an actual human?

No, it's just that upbeat On-Hold Man again.

"Thank you for continuing to hold," he says. "While we do have an unusually high call volume at this time, we value your call. Please hold for the next available associate."

You've heard this message so many times, you've memorized it. You hate On-Hold Man. You want to strangle him.

You curse. You rage. But what's the use? You sigh and settle into the quiet desperation of waiting. Foolishly, you begin to contemplate how much of your life has been spent waiting.

Waiting at the post office, where the clerks seem to move in slow motion. Or at the supermarket, where everybody in the ten-items-or-less line is shooting death-ray glances at the guy with twelve items.

Thank you for continuing to hold. ...

"Waiting is an insult to us," says anthropologist David Murray. "We feel we're being put down when we're forced to wait.

We sense that we've been disrespected; hence, the anger."

We are a busy people. We have day-planners and lists of Things to Do Today. We're highly caffeinated, and we expect life to be full of action, bing, bang, boom. We see waiting as time taken from life, Murray says, while other cultures see it as a part of life.

"We feel we are living only during an event—the rest of the time we're hibernating," he says. "It's a particularly American or Western attitude. In nonindustrial tribal societies, the rhythms are slower and waiting is part of life. In the absence of clocks and hard-and-fast punctual expectations, it's hard to be frustrated by waiting."

Several years ago, Polish journalist Ryszard Kapuscinski was stuck in a Siberian airport for four days, waiting out a blizzard, bored out of his skull. "It is a dreadful sort of idleness, and unbearable tedium to sit motionless like this," he wrote. "But on the other hand, don't millions and millions of people the world over pass the time in just such a passive way. And haven't they done so for years, for centuries?"

You recall a statistic reprinted everywhere a few years back, attributed to a Pittsburgh research firm called Priority

Management. Americans spend five years of their lives waiting in lines.

For a seventy-five-year-long life. It comes out to more than 1 1/2 hours a day.

Can that possibly be true?

There are other statistics: on an average day, according to a book called *On an Average Day* by Tom Heymann, Americans spend 101,369,863 hours waiting in line. That's 37 billion hours a year.

And that's just waiting in line. But waiting is a many-splendored thing. Waiting for the weekend. Waiting for the Messiah. Waiting for the waiter. Waiting for your ship to come in. Waiting for takeoff. Waiting with baited breath. Waiting for a phone call.

There's the intense waiting of childhood. Waiting for Christmas morning. Waiting for the last day of school. Waiting through endless car trips: are we there yet?

Waiting to grow whiskers. Waiting to grow breasts. Waiting to grow up.

There's the bittersweet waiting of romance and procreation. Waiting for her to notice you. Waiting for him to ask you out. Waiting for her to get ready. Waiting for him to pop the question. Waiting for your period. Waiting for the results of your pregnancy test. Waiting through your ninth month of pregnancy, which seems as long as the previous eight combined.

Some waiting is more painful. Waiting for the jury to reach a verdict. Waiting for biopsy results. Waiting in refugee camps. Waiting in prison. Waiting for your teenager, and it's two in the morning, and she hasn't called.

... we have an unusually high call volume at this time ...

The poor wait more than the rich.

They wait in soup lines and welfare lines and unemployment lines. They wait in emergency rooms and free medical clinics. They cannot pay with money, so they pay with time—little chunks of their lives.

The poor wait for buses and subways while the rich zoom past in cars or glide by in limousines driven by chauffeurs who are waiting and ready to open the door when their bosses appear.

Once, Louis XIV stepped out of his palace to find his royal driver just arriving in the royal coach. The king was unhappy. "I almost had to wait," he grumbled.

"If you have enough money, you can buy someone else's time." says psychologist Robert Levine. "You can pay people to run your errands. Your time is worth more than their time."

In his book *A Geography of Time*, Levine codified what he calls "The Rules of the Waiting Game." One rule was, Status dictates who waits: the higher your rank, the more people you can keep waiting—and the longer you can keep them waiting.

When the company president wants to see you, you hustle to his office. Then he keeps you waiting, watching his secretary make phone calls for him. He's too important to wait for someone to answer. So she gets them on the phone and says, Please hold for Mr. Smith.

It's nothing personal, just a reminder of who's boss. And it's nothing new. In the Middle Ages, Pope Gregory VII is said to have forced Henry IV, the Holy Roman emperor who had challenged his authority, to stand barefoot in the snow for three days before meeting with him. In 1949, Joseph Stalin kept Mao Zedong waiting for 17 days in a dacha in the freezing Russian winter. Mao had just taken over China, but Stalin was showing him who was boss in the Communist world.

But you don't have to be a pope or a dictator to play the game. Clerks enjoy this, too, when they make you wait in line and then suddenly hang up a sign that says "Closed" and amble off.

"Making a person wait is an exercise in power." Levine says, "There is no greater symbol of domination, since time is the only possession which can in no sense be replaced."

... we value your call ...

The biggest controversy is whether one long serpentine line or many short lines is better. This is serious for businesses: should you line people up in one long line, like they do at most banks? Or in many short lines, like they do in supermarkets? Single lines look longer, which can scare customers away. But multiple lines can frustrate customers who watch as people who arrived after them get served before them.

"When somebody slips by you, your psychological cost is high," says MIT professor Richard Larson, who has created computer systems to help airlines, banks and department stores deal with their line problems.

"You're going to remember that. And maybe next time you'll go to a place with a long serpentine line."

But Ziv Carmon, a professor of consumer psychology at Duke University, says some businesses—fast-food restaurants with nearby competitors, for instance—should use multiple lines because they look shorter.

... Please hold for the next available associate.

We keep creating products to eliminate delay, but we're still bedeviled by waiting. "As our pace of life gets more hectic, our tolerance for waiting in line goes down," Larson says.

Obviously, we've got a problem.

We got tired of waiting in restaurants, so we invented fast-food joints. We got too impatient to wait for conventional ovens to cook our meals, so we invented microwave ovens to cook them faster.

Now we grumble about the lines in fast-food restaurants. We stand in front of our microwave wondering why it's so slow. We grouse about how long it takes the computer to boot up. Every time-saving device allows us to put more on our schedule, which makes us more obsessed with time and less tolerant of waiting.

UNDERSTANDING DESCRIPTIVE DETAILS

A. Answer these questions. Underline the details in the reading that support your answer.

Mark the question number in the margin.

1. According to the author, how do people feel when they are waiting on hold?

   _____

2. How does the author describe North American attitudes toward waiting?

   _____

3. How does the author describe the kind of waiting that the poor do?

   _____

4. How does the author describe a company president's way of making people wait?

   _____

5. Give the details for two historical examples of people who were kept waiting.

   a. _____

   b. _____

Work with a partner to ask and answer the questions. Compare the information you underlined.

B. Give three examples of the following ideas from the reading in note form.

1. Waiting for something that will happen in time

   a. _____

   b. _____

   c. _____

2. Waiting for something when we are children

   a. _____

   b. _____

   c. _____

3. Waiting for something when we are in love or having children

   a. _____

   b. _____

   c. _____

4. Waiting for something that is painful

   a. _____

   b. _____

   c. _____

Work with a partner to check your answers. Refer to the reading to confirm the information.

UNDERSTANDING FACTS AND OPINIONS

■ **READING TIP:**
Remember that facts are information that can be supported by evidence or by the work of an expert and opinions are information that are an interpretation of or a point of view about certain facts.

A. Read the following statements from the article. Write *F* if the information is factual or *O* if it expresses the author's opinion.

1. _____ "Waiting is an insult to us," says anthropologist David Murray.

2. _____ You recall a statistic reprinted everywhere a few years back, attributed to a research firm called Priority Management: Americans spend five years of their lives waiting in lines.

3. _____ The poor wait for buses and subways while the rich zoom past in cars or glide by in limousines . . .

4. _____ "If you have enough money, you can buy someone else's time," says psychologist Robert Levine.

B. Choose two more examples of fact and opinion statements in the reading. Highlight these statements and mark *F* or *O* in the margin. Compare your answers with those of a partner or with others in a small group. Give the reasons for your answers.

APPLYING THE INFORMATION

Interview: How much can you fit into a day?

What are the important daily activities that you try to fit into a typical day?

1. Make a list of these activities.
2. Estimate the amount of time that you spend on each activity during the day.
3. Compare your list with the information that follows.

USA TODAY

Making every minute count

By Kim Painter

Life goes faster and gets more action-packed. But a day still has just 24 hours. How we spend them, at least according to a variety of researchers cited in *Faster: The Acceleration of Just About Everything:*

7 hours and 18 minutes asleep — a 20 percent drop from a century ago.

6 hours working, if we're employed.

4 hours doing housework, if we're women, less than half of that if we're men.

3 hours watching TV — double the 1965 figure.

1 hour and 26 minutes on line, if we're on-line computer users.

1 hour eating.

52 minutes on the phone.

41 minutes reading magazines and newspapers.

29 minutes visiting other people.

31 minutes caring for children.

16 minutes searching for lost objects.

16 minutes reading books.

7 minutes caring for pets and plants.

4 minutes having sex—the same amount the government says we spend filling out government forms.

Don't bother to do the math, says author James Gleick. it will just prove what we all know: There aren't enough hours in a day.

A few *Faster* facts:

The USA had no official standard time until the end of World War I. Now, some computer users are so obsessed with the exact time that they maintain a constant linkup with the government's atomic clocks at the Directorate of Time in Washington, D.C.

The Japanese have invented an elevator that goes 40 feet per second — "a good climb rate for an airplane."

In 1984, Americans bought 80,000 fax machines; by 1989, it was 2 million and rising.

The average sound bite by a presidential candidate on a network news show lasted more than 40 seconds in 1968; by 1988, it was 10 seconds and dropping.

4. Do you think you try to fit too many activities into your daily life? Can you make better use of your time?

5. Based on the information from the reading and on ideas of your own, make a list of five questions about how we do or don't have control over our time. Interview two students and write their answers in note form.

Interview Questions	*Student A*	*Student B*
1.		
2.		
3.		
4.		
5.		

Discuss your interviews with others in a small group.

Vocabulary Building

WORD FORMS

When the ending *-ist, -or*, or *-er* is added to a noun, the new noun can be used to refer to a person. For example, by adding *-ist* to the word "biology," we have biologist, a person who works or studies in this field.

A. Scan the readings and find examples of words ending in *-ist*, *-or*, or *-er* that refer to people. Write the noun and give a definition in your own words.

Noun	Adjective
1. _____	_____
2. _____	_____
3. _____	_____
4. _____	_____
5. _____	_____

B. Write the noun or adjective form of the following words.

Noun	Adjective
1. _____	biological
2. _____	depressing
3. _____	essential
4. _____	natural
5. information	_____
6. insult	_____
7. convenience	_____

8. _____   intense

9. _____   tolerant

Write three sentences using a different noun and adjective in each. Work with a partner to check your answers.

Vocabulary in Context

You can often understand the meaning of a new word from your understanding of the other words in the sentence.

Complete each sentence with one of the following verbs. Provide the correct tense and form of the verb. Underline the words in the sentence that helped you make your choice.

a. boast   b. challenge   c. contemplate   d. dictate   e. hustle
f. recognize   g. speculate   h. take over

1. The coach told the players to _____ if they wanted to get to the game on time.

2. We needed time to _____ how we were going to solve this very complicated problem.

3. The researchers could only _____ about the possible reasons for the results they had found.

4. It didn't take them long to _____ that there was too much work for them to do in the time they had left.

5. The class felt so proud of their work that they _____ that they would be the first-place winners.

6. She _____ the class to find the answer to a very difficult problem.

7. I'd like you to _____ the driving if I get too tired to continue.

8. She is in a position to _____ the rules that the teams will play by.

Check your answers. Work with a partner and read the sentences to each other. Together, find three other unusual words or phrases in the readings. Circle these and use them in sentences of your own.

Expanding Your Language

SPEAKING

A. Oral Presentation: Choose a topic related to time. Some examples are the different types of calendars that are used all over the world, the different types of clocks and other ways of keeping time that are used, or the problem of jet lag and how to avoid it when you travel across different time zones. To prepare your presentation, follow these steps.

1. Choose your topic for a three minute presentation.
2. On your own, brainstorm an outline of the important ideas you want to talk about.
3. Discuss your ideas with another person. Ask for suggestions for ideas to include or exclude.
4. Gather information from your school library or from the Internet or from your own sources to complete your outline.
5. Repeat step 3. Show your completed outline to your teacher.
6. Practice delivering your presentation until you are comfortable explaining without reading your notes.
7. Make your presentation to others in a small group.

The Time Capsule: At times, people decide to collect items that tell important things about themselves and their world to people in future generations. They put these things in a container so that many years later, long after they are dead, a record of the times they lived in will exist for people to study.

B. Group Work—Imagine that you are on a committee to select the items to put into a time capsule. Working with others in a small group, decide on a list of seven items to include. Prepare your list to present to others. Also prepare to discuss the reasons for your choices.

WRITING

Topic Writing: Write about how our experience of time has changed based on your discussions and the chapter readings. Follow these steps:

1. Outline ideas about the nature of time in different periods, including both the positive and negative impact on people's lives.

The Past

Before and After the   *Advantages and Disadvantages*
Industrial Revolution

_____   _____

_____   _____

_____   _____

_____   _____

The Present

Computer Age

_____   _____

_____   _____

_____   _____

_____   _____

Future Predictions

_____   _____

_____   _____

_____   _____

_____   _____

2. Write three or four sentences about

   a. the nature of time in the past.

   b. the positive and negative points of this time.

   c. the nature of time in the computer age.

   d. the positive and negative points of this time.

   e. your prediction about the nature of time in the future.

3. Write about each time period in a separate paragraph.

In writing, remember to:

- Indent at the beginning of the paragraph.
- Explain the ideas in complete sentences.
- Organize the sentences in logical sequence.

Give your writing to your teacher for feedback.

Reaction Writing: Write your reactions to the ideas that you read about in this chapter concerning time and the pace of life today. What thoughts did you have about the information or in the group discussions that followed?

CHAPTER 6

Procrastination: Can We Manage Our Time?

Chapter Openers

MATCHING MEANINGS

Match each word with the definition that fits it best.

_____ 1. Procrastinator   a. to put off doing something until a later date

_____ 2. Procrastinate   b. person who repeatedly delays completing his or her work

_____ 3. Postpone   c. to continually delay doing something that we don't want to do

Check your answers with a partner. Use each of these words in an example. Which is worse, to procrastinate or to postpone?

DISCUSSION QUESTIONS

Think about the following questions. Share your ideas with a partner or with a small group.

1. Why do people procrastinate? List three important reasons.

   a. _____

   b. _____

   c. _____

2. Is procrastination a serious problem? Give three examples to support your opinion.

   a. _____

   b. _____

   c. _____

3. What can procrastinators do to solve their problems? Give three solutions.

   a. _____

   b. _____

   c. _____

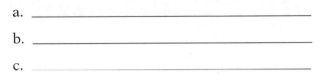

Exploring and Understanding Reading

PREDICTING

This reading is about a study that looked at the health effects of procrastinating. Before you read, think about what kind of information you could expect to learn from this type of article. In the following list, check (✔) the ideas you think you'll find in the reading.

1. _____ The health benefits of procrastination

2. _____ The facts about procrastination and stress

3. _____ The type of people involved in the study

4. _____ The effect procrastination has on people's work

5. _____ The importance of research on future studies on procrastination

6. _____ The importance of research to science

7. _____ Stories about why researchers chose to do this study

Compare the items you checked with those a partner checked. Discuss the reasons for the ideas you checked and those you didn't.

Quickly read the selection and look for the ideas you checked. Add to or change your predictions.

Probing Procrastination

By the editors of *Science*

We all suspected that procrastination was bad for us. Now comes research to prove that it may actually be unhealthy, too.

In what they claim is the first experimental study of its kind, social psychologists Dianne M. Tice and Roy F. Baumeister at Case Western Reserve University in Cleveland report in the November issue of *Psychological Science* that procrastinators suffer from more stress and health problems.

One study asked forty-four students in a health psychology course to fill out daily symptom checklists and weekly measures of stress and work requirements for a month. Self-reported procrastinators handed in their papers later than nonprocrastinators; they also got lower grades. A second study of sixty students revealed that by the end of the term, procrastinators experienced more stress and reported more health symptoms such as colds and flu.

Interestingly, procrastination does work to some extent: Its practitioners actually reported less stress and fewer health symptoms earlier in the term than did those who had their noses to the grindstone. But self-indulgence takes its toll.

"Procrastinators end up suffering more and performing worse than other people," the authors conclude. They say the study helps place procrastination in the realm of behaviors, such as drug abuse, marked by impulsivity and "poor self-regulation,"

Procrastination researcher Joseph R. Ferrari of DePaul University in Chicago says the Tice study provides "evidence we haven't had before." he notes, though, that the study subjects were only simple "academic" procrastinators—and not necessarily "chronic procrastinators," who suffer from a life-disrupting problem.

Such research is important for designing more effective treatments for procrastination, says Timothy Pychl, who heads the Procrastination Research Group at Carleton University in Ottawa. "They run clinics on every campus in North America for people who procrastinate," he says. The main approach is "time management," but researchers agree it's not very effective and that serious procrastinators have deeper problems, such as depression and low self-esteem, that need to be addressed.

–Science

UNDERSTANDING DETAILS IN A STUDY

Most reports of studies contain certain types of information: the type of study, the author(s) of the study, the subjects (people who participated in the study), the purpose, the results, and its importance. Complete this report form. Write the key information in note form.

REPORT ON PROCRASTINATION STUDIES

Background

Purpose of research: _____

Overall results of research: _____

Author of study: _____

Study No. 1

Subjects: _____

What information was collected and when: _____

_____

Results: _____

Study No. 2

Subjects: _____

What information was collected and when: _____

_____

Results: _____

Reports from procrastinators: _____

Discussion of Results

1. What has been learned: _____

2. Limitations of the studies: _____

_____

3. Importance of the research: _____

Work with a partner. Using your notes, take turns explaining the information in the important sections of the report.

After Reading

APPLYING INFORMATION; SOLVING A PROBLEM

How do you feel when you are managing your time well? In the first reading, "Probing Procrastination" you learned that there are two kinds of procrastinators, chronic—or serious—procrastinators and "academic" procrastinators, who supposedly have a less serious problem. In the readings that follow, you'll look for a few suggestions on how procrastinators can be helped.

PAIRED READINGS

Choose either Reading 1, which follows, or Reading 2, which is found in the Exercise section on page E–2. These articles contain advice about how to stop getting behind in work.

Help! I'm a Procrastinator

Q: *I wait until the eleventh hour to begin any project. How can I change this stress-producing habit?*

A: Procrastination is a widespread time-management problem that often arises when a task seems difficult or overpowering. Almost everyone at one time or another engages in task avoidance—putting things off until tomorrow, and then, when tomorrow comes, putting them off again until another tomorrow or even the day after.

If you find yourself excessively procrastinating, spinning your wheels and getting nowhere in a hurry, some of these strategies should help you manage the problem: • **Make a list** of everything you have to do; set priorities and select one project to focus on. • **Plan ahead.** Don't rely on inspiration alone; you've got to make a move to get things done. • **Write an intention statement** and set specific but realistic goals. • **Break the task into small segments.** You can bring any task down to size and make it less intimidating by devoting 20 or 30 minutes a day to working on it. • **Schedule your tasks.** Devote a set time to work on each project regularly. • **Delegate.** If you don't have to do it all yourself, ask someone else to do part of the job. You'll still feel a sense of accomplishment. • **Promise yourself a reward** on completion. • **Estimate the amount of time** you think it will take to complete a task, then increase the time allocated by 100 percent.

–Essence

GIVING ADVICE; LOOKING FOR TIPS

■ READING TIP:
The use of graphics (points or bullets) and boldface type helps the reader locate tips in a reading quickly.

Prepare to report on the tips you find in the reading. Follow these steps:

1. Skim the article and highlight the tips you find.

2. Make a list of some of the tips.

_____

_____

_____

_____

_____

_____

RECAPPING THE INFORMATION

Work with a partner who read the *same information* and compare your list.

RETELLING THE INFORMATION

Work with a partner who read *different information*. Together, use your tip list to make a new list that contains the information from both lists. Do not repeat any ideas. Decide the best order for the information in your tip list.

_____

_____

_____

_____

_____

Can these suggestions help the types of procrastinators in the reading "Probing Procrastination"?

REACTING TO THE INFORMATION; STRESS AND TIME MANAGEMENT

You have read that procrastinators have increased health problems due to stress and that experts have advice for people with time management problems like procrastination.

Think about the following questions. Share your ideas with others in a small group.

- Why do you think people procrastinate?
- What is the most useful advice for procrastinators?
- Do you think all stress is bad, or can some stress be useful? What is the difference between these two types?
- When do you know that procrastination has become a problem for you?

Vocabulary Building

VOCABULARY IN CONTEXT

Matching: General Information and Specific Facts

In English, general information given in one sentence or clause is often followed by sentences or clauses that contain specific facts about—or examples of—that general idea. Often, the language used in the examples helps you understand the ideas in the general statement and vice-versa.

Match each general sentence in Column A with one that best follows from Column B

Column A

_____ 1. Social psychologists report that procrastinators suffer from more stress and health problems.

_____ 2. Procrastination works to some extent.

_____ 3. Serious procrastinators have deeper problems.

_____ 4. They run clinics on every campus in North America for people who procrastinate.

Column B

a. The main approach is time management but researchers agree it's not very effective.

b. Some actually reported less stress and fewer health problems earlier in the term.

c. A study revealed that procrastinators experienced more stress and reported more health symptoms such as colds and flu.

d. such as depression and low self-esteem, that need to be addressed.

Check your answers. Work with a partner to read the pairs of sentences.

Signal Words That Introduce Examples

There are words or phrases that are often used to introduce examples. One of these is *such* or *such as*.

Scan the reading "Probing Procrastination" and circle the uses of *such* or *such as*. Then, in the chart that follows, list the idea and the examples that *such* or *such as* introduces.

	Idea	*Example*
1.		
2.		
3.		
4.		

Expanding Your Language

SPEAKING

Exploring a Different Point of View: the Advantages of Procrastination

Is procrastination always a bad thing? Some people might argue otherwise. The reading that follows makes a few humorous points.

A. Skim the reading and find three advantages that you think are valid (believable or true in your opinion or experience); find two that you think aren't.

Procrastinate Now

(Original title: Here's Something to Read While You're Not Doing Your Taxes)

By Barbara Brotman

The arrival of spring can mean only one thing: It's time to bring the clay planters inside for the winter. It was supposed to be done six months ago, but blind adherence to a sensible chore schedule is not the way of a practitioner of the art of procrastination.

And art it is. Oh, certainly there are dilettantes who dabble in the field, keeping a few unpacked boxes from the last move in the basement or maintaining a modest slush pile of junk mail. But some of us have achieved a higher level of accomplishment in the field of putting off accomplishment. Is it not time to stop upbraiding us with brisk announcements of official desk-cleaning days, and give us credit for the complex delaying tactics we use to avoid answering mail for months at a time?

Never mind the psychological explanations unearthed by scientists—fear of failure, fear of success, perfectionism, avoidance of conflict or over-reliance on chore completion as a source of self-esteem. ("I pick up the dry cleaning on time, therefore I am good.")

And don't call us lazy; researchers say that laziness is a minor factor because procrastination is so time-consuming. A social worker who led procrastination counseling groups estimates 75 percent of procrastinators' work time was spent putting off the work.

Why not consider the advantages of procrastination?

• Improved efficiency. If you keep putting off a chore, you may not have to do it at all. Someone else may do your chore or it may become a moot point, streamlining your to-do list while giving you less to do.

Take storm windows. In our guest room, ours are leaning against the wall because we never got around to putting them in for the winter. Now we don't have to. All we have to do is put them away until next winter. Although, frankly—why bother?

Or let's say you owe someone a letter. If you wait long enough, the person may die, pointed out the pasha of postponement, Les Waas, president of the Procrastinators Club of America (bumper sticker: "Procrastinate NOW"). Or you may die, in which case only the most churlish could still hold a grudge.

Moreover, you can do things faster if you put them off, because you have to. Most people take three months to complete their income-tax returns, Waas observed; procrastinators take three hours on April 15.

"A positive procrastinator is . . . better organized than the average individual," said Waas, an advertising agency owner who founded the club on a lark in 1956 and then found himself getting applications for membership. "Many of the things we put off never have to be done anyway. You save a lot of time."

• Simplicity. What better way to pare your life down to the essentials than to put off cleaning out your refrigerator?

Let those newspapers and school notices pile up, and repeat: Ommm . . .

• Preservation of mental health. If we completed all our minor tasks promptly, we would be left with too much time on our hands to consider our major problems, the meaning of life and what to do when our children become teenagers. Idle hands make mental mischief, but procrastinating hands always have photographs to file.

• Excitement. Can anything truly compare with the thrill of a last-minute panic? Desperation focuses the mind and jump-starts the creative process.

Cleaning the fishbowl at midnight to avoid imminent piscine death, buying birthday gifts at the all-night drugstore, vacuuming dust bunnies 15 minutes before guests arrive—these are the things that make the blood course and the mouth swear.

In short, we are to be envied, not reproached. Join us in our off-putting ways, and you, too, can truly taste life, and the bittersweet tang of late-payment fees.

B. Highlight the advantages of procrastination in note form. In the margin, write *V* if you think it is valid, and *NV* if you think it isn't.

Compare your answers with a partner. Be prepared to discuss the reasons for your choices.

C. What makes a piece of writing fun to read? How do you know that the writer is joking? Reread the selection and highlight phrases or ideas that you think are funny. Work with a partner to confirm your ideas. Be prepared to discuss your ideas with others.

Managing Your Time

Stephen Covey is a noted author and speaker on the subject of time management. In his opinion, it is important to decide your priorities according to the goals you set for yourself. Only then will you be able to address the question of how to avoid procrastination.

Covey suggests that you analyze the activities in your life so that you first focus on those that most further your goals. The following grid reflects Covey's advice to categorize demands on your time into those that are urgent, important, unimportant, and not urgent. See the grid for examples and add some examples of your own.

To complete an analysis of your time management, follow these steps:

- Record your daily schedule for one week.
- Think about your goals for the next period of time—one semester, one year, or more.
- Write a list of these goals.
- Examine your activities with these goals in mind. Write the activities in the part of the grid where they belong.

The Time Management Matrix

	Urgent	Not urgent
Important	I. Activities: *meeting a deadline*	II. Activities *exercising regularly*
Not important	III. Activities: *answering the phone*	IV. Activities *watching TV*

Adapted from *The Seven Habits of Highly Effective People*, Stephen Covey

Discuss what you wrote with others in a small group. Talk about what this analysis has shown you about how much your goals and your activities coincide or not.

WRITING

Reaction Writing: Write in your journal about the topic of procrastination and time management. How do you feel you manage your time? What do you want to be doing in the next year? In two years? In five years?

Read On: Taking It Further

A DIFFERENT POINT OF VIEW

Madonna sings "This used to be my playground" in a song about her memories of the past. Imagine that you were to return to your childhood home. What would you expect to find? The following reading is a very personal story of one woman's return to her childhood home after an absence of many years.

A. Read the story and prepare to discuss the following questions.

■ How does the writer describe the effects that the passage of time has had on her childhood home?

■ What are the feelings that she experienced returning to her childhood home?

■ What does this story tell us about the nature of time?

THE NEW YORK TIMES

A Sentimental Journey To La Casa of Childhood

By Mirta Ojito

HAVANA, Feb. 1 — This is the moment when, in my dreams, I begin to cry. And yet, I'm strangely calm as I go up the stairs to the apartment of my childhood in Santos Suárez, the only place that, after all these years, I still refer to as la casa, home.

I am holding a pen and a reporter's notebook in my hand and, as I always do when I am working, I count the steps: twenty. In my memory, there were only sixteen. The staircase seems narrower than I remember, the ceiling lower.

Perhaps I have grown taller, perhaps my hips have widened with age and pregnancy. I am buying mental time, distracting my mind from what I am certain will be a shock.

After seventeen years and eight months, I have returned to Cuba as a reporter. I am here to cover the visit of Pope John Paul II, not to cry at the sight of a chipped, old tile on the floor.

The last time I went down these steps I was sixteen years old and a police car was waiting for me and my family downstairs. They had come to tell us that my uncle, like thousands of other cuban exiles who had returned to Cuba to claim their relatives, waited at the port of Mariel to take us to Miami in a leased shrimp boat.

It was May 7, 1980, the first days of what became known as the Mariel boat lift, the period from April to September 1980 when more than 125,000 Cubans left the island for the United States.

That day I left my house in a hurry. The police gave us ten minutes to get ready and pack the few personal items we were allowed to take: an extra set of clothing, some pictures, toothbrushes. Everything else, from my books to my dolls and my parents' wedding china, remained behind. There were dishes in the sink and food in the refrigerator. My underwear in a drawer and my mother's sewing machine open for work.

Since then, I have often thought about this house, remembering every detail, every curve and tile and squeaky sound. The green walls of the living room, the view from the balcony, the feel of the cold tiles under my bare feet, the sound of my father's key in the keyhole and the muffled noise from the old refrigerator in the kitchen.

A stranger opens the door and I tell her who I am and what I want. "I used to live here," I say. "I'd like to take a look."

Surprisingly, she knows my name. She asks if I am the older or the younger child who used to live in the house. I say I am the older as I look over her head. Straight into my past. My home remains practically as we left it, seemingly frozen in time, like much of Cuba today.

This is a strange feeling. I knew I would face my childhood by coming here, but I never expected to relive it as I am doing now. I go out to the balcony and then, as if on cue, I hear someone calling out my childhood nickname, "Mirtica! Mirtica!"

For a moment, I do not know who is calling or even if the call is real. It sounds like my mother calling me for dinner. But it is the neighbor from the corner who looked up from her terrace and somehow recognized me. I wave faintly. I want to stay in this apartment for a long time. I want to be left alone, but I cannot. It is no longer my home.

I knew this would be an emotional visit. Before I mustered enough courage to go up to the apartment, I had walked through the neighborhood. As my father asked me to do, I visit la bodega and search for Juan, the Spaniard who once owned it and, after it was confiscated by the Government in the early years of the revolution, remained there as an employee of the state.

He is retired now, but I find him helping out at another bodega, and we chat. I take a picture for my father as he stands behind the counter with a pencil balanced behind his ear, as he always did.

I walk the streets and find faces I recognize. I approach some; others approach me because, they tell me, I remind them of my mother. Some even call out her name, which is also mine, from across the street: "Mirta, what are you doing here? You've come back?"

They tell me who died and who left. The son of my sixth-grade teacher lost a leg in a bicycle accident. My next-door neighbor left for Spain with her son, Pepito, to claim an inheritance. The musician from downstairs died of bone cancer; his daughter married an Italian and left.

After a second visit to the apartment, I leave. And I leave exactly the way I left almost 18 years ago, profoundly sad, surrounded by friends and neighbors, people glad that I remembered them, unselfish people who are happy that I left and live better than they do.

Who says that Cubans are divided by politics or even by an ocean? In Enamorados Street, at the foot of a small hill called San Julio, my home and my people remain.

■ **READING TIP:**
Don't forget to write your reading journal and vocabulary log entries in your notebook.

B. Write your reactions to this story in your reading journal. Can you imagine yourself in a similar situation? What would you expect to find? How would you feel?

UNIT 4

Technology Matters

The danger of the past was that men became slaves.
The danger of the future is that men may become robots.

— *Erich Fromm*

Introducing the Topics

It would be very hard to imagine life without machines. We use them to wash, dry, cook, clean, entertain, . . . and think. This unit will focus on the "thinking" machine—the computer. Chapter 7 will look at robots and what they can and cannot do. Chapter 8 is about shopping on the Internet.

Points of Interest

ANALYZING OUR NEEDS

School, health, work, and leisure are different areas of our lives. In the chart that follows, make a list of examples of ways in which a computer can be used.

School	Health	Work	Leisure
		employee records	

Share your examples with a partner or in a small group. Is the computer an essential item for all these areas? In which is it just a luxury? Why? Using your examples to help you, discuss what the consequences would be in each area if suddenly all the computers broke down.

WHAT IS YOUR OPINION? AGREE OR DISAGREE

Circle *A* if you agree or *D* if you disagree with the following statements.

1. A   D   We are much less sociable because of computers.

2. A   D   Computers have caused our brains to slow down.

3. A   D   Computers give us time to focus on more important things.

4. A   D   We have become overdependent on computers.

5. A   D   Computers will one day have the same kind of intelligence as humans.

Work with a partner or in a small group. Compare your ideas. Explain your ideas using reasons and examples.

CHAPTER 7

Robots—Machines That Can Think and Feel

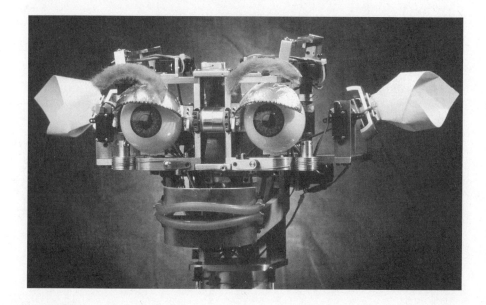

Chapter Openers

DEFINITIONS

Work with a partner or in a small group. Agree on a definition for each of the following terms. Do *not* use a dictionary.

- Intelligence _____

    _____

- Emotion _____

    _____

■ Robot _____

_____

Discuss the characteristics of a robot that is (a) intelligent, (b) capable of feeling.

PERSONALIZING

Imagine that you could design your own robot. What four things would you like it to be able to do?

1. _____

2. _____

3. _____

4. _____

What four things would you never expect it to do?

1. *Convince the children to go to bed.* _____

2. _____

3. _____

4. _____

Understanding and Exploring Reading

The idea of robots has been around for quite a while and has gone through periods of being both popular and unpopular. What period is it going through now?

SKIMMING

Quickly read the following article and find the answer to the preceding question.

COX NEWS SERVICE

Even Sony's Betting on a Robotic Future

By Bill Husted

1. Years ago, when science-fiction novels—not video games—were an obsession with most boys and some girls, the robot was king.

2. The robots of science fiction were wonderful (and sometimes awful) creatures that could think for themselves and that seemed like mechanical versions of a real person. For a time, it seemed almost certain that—as technology moved to the stage where such things were possible—robot housekeepers and waiters would be common by the end of the twentieth century.

3. Then the wind shifted and robots—that kind of robot—became less popular. Sure there were robots, but these were the computerized cutting and welding arms used in automobile manufacturing, designed to do one specialized task. There were also toy robots—even expensive ones—that could wander around in an amusing way but served no real purpose.

4. Well, for all of you who grew up and dreamed of someday having a robot of your own, there is hope from an unlikely source: Sony.

5. Here is what happened. Sony built a $2,500 robotic dog, AIBO. It looked like a dog, had some ability to learn and could even be taken for a walk on a leash. Each dog has its own personality. (It took one owner three months to teach his dog how to walk).

6. Sony was shocked when it sold 2,000 of those creatures in the United States and also thousands in Japan. So it came out with another 10,000 for the United States Within one month, 135,000 applicants entered a lottery to win ownership of one.

7. Now, Sony thinks there is a future for real robots—for household helpers and for industrial robots to be used in mines.

8. The importance of this news is not that some company thinks it can turn a buck selling robots. The importance is that this is Sony—these are people who make a living selling popular technology, not strange one-ofs that are too expensive and too specialized.

9. Here is the real surprise. A quote from Toshi Doi, president of Sony Digital Creatures Laboratory (from an interview with Reuters): "In the future the total industry of automated robots will exceed the total amount of personal-computer industry."

10. If Doi is right, then there is definitely a robot in your future.

TELLBACK: TO DISCUSS

■ **READING TIP:**
Tellback means to talk about information you have just read without looking back at it.

Work with a partner. Talk about the article you have just skimmed by answering the following questions orally. Take turns and do *not* look at the article.

1. What kinds of robots were being predicted by science fiction writers in the past?

2. What types of robots were actually produced?

3. What did Sony build?

4. How successful was it?

5. What is being predicted now for the future of robots?

After you have finished, look back at the article and check your answers together.

PREDICTING USING PREVIOUS KNOWLEDGE

The following reading is about household robots. Work with a partner or in a small group. Using the previous reading and what you know about robots, predict the answers to these questions.

1. What household tasks could robots perform?
2. How soon will household robots be available?
3. What skills will these robots need in order to carry out their tasks?
4. How much will they cost?
5. What age group will benefit the most?

SKIMMING/TELLING BACK TO FIND IMPORTANT INFORMATION

■ *READING TIP:*
Newspaper articles often have very short paragraphs. No one paragraph completely provides all the details about one main idea.

Work with a partner. Break the article into four parts—each part consisting of approximately ten paragraphs. Skim each part and tell each other what you remember *without* looking back at the article.

HARTFORD COURANT

The Robot of the House

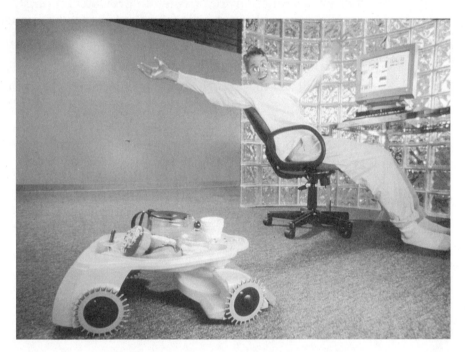

Vast advances in the power of computer chips have enabled robotics researchers to build machines that are capable of thinking on their feet. Coming soon, to a kitchen near you:

By John Moran

1. When they married nearly two decades ago, Hans Moravec promised his wife that one day he'd get her a robot to vacuum the house.

2. He's expecting to deliver on that promise one day soon.

3. Moravec, a professor at Pittsburgh's Carnegie Mellon University, says the pace of progress in robotics-research labs suggests that household robots might become commercially available in five to ten years.

4. "Robots have started doing things all over the place," said Moravec. "The performance is just astronomically above what it was in the seventies and eighties, when we could barely make a computer cross a room," he said.

5. Robots of a sort have already been working for some time in industrial settings. Often, they're single-function devices that simply pick up a piece of material to move it, or spot-weld two pieces of metal together.

6. But such robots are so limited in capability and function that many don't even consider them worthy of being called robots.

7. "Most of the things that are out in the world that call themselves robots are not," said Jake Mendelssohn, a professor at Hartford, Conn., Trinity College.

8. To Mendelssohn—and plenty of other robot-fanciers—a bucket of bolts just isn't a robot until it can perceive its environment and automatically respond.

9. No remote control by humans allowed.

10. To function in the "real world"—that is, in the varied and changing environments of home and office—robots have to be much, much smarter than remote controlled machinery. They have to be able to see the environment and respond to any changes that happen.

11. From that point of view, even the most sophisticated robot seemed as stupid as a stone.

12. For most of the past two decades, that hurdle seemed insurmountable. The technical challenges of designing a robot that could see and respond to the environment were overwhelming.

13. In recent years, though, vast advances in the power of computer chips have enabled robotics researchers to build machines that are capable of thinking on their feet.

14. "Things are moving a lot faster here lately with the computer capabilities that are being developed," said Gene Ronan, technical editor of *Robot Science and Technology* magazine.

15. By one estimate, today's top personal-computer chips have the capacity to process information on a par with the brain of an insect or goldfish.

16. As a result, the latest experimental robots can quickly identify obstacles and calculate a way around them.

17. They can map entire rooms and then scan them again later to determine whether anything has moved or whether something new has been introduced.

18. Quite simply, none of the tasks that humans would most like robots to perform —from cleaning bathrooms to taking out the trash—would be possible without that skill.

19. Moravec said progress in robotics will put robots into common use within the next decade or so.

20. The first wave, he said, will be a new generation of industrial robots that move more easily through warehouses, office buildings and the like.

21. They will be followed by a second wave of single-purpose consumer robots for vacuuming and mowing.

22. In a third generation, the home robots would have a movable arm that could pick up things, carry things and even wash things.

23. Although most consumer-oriented robots are still being refined in the labs, a few have begun making their way into the marketplace, showing the tantalizing potential of self-guided machines.

24. One is Cye. Cye is a 10-pound cyber-creature that can't cook dinner or do the laundry yet, but can do a number of other domestic skills. It can push a little wagon with a tray of food and drink and bring the dirty dishes to the kitchen.

25. Cye can also push a vacuum cleaner, and even greet visitors at the door and lead them back to the family room. And when it is finished with the daily tasks, Cye rolls back to its home base and recharges itself.

26. It comes in three different colors and sells for about $900.

27. Another is the AutoMower, a battery-driven lawnmower that will trim your grass, untouched by human hands.

28. The AutoMower uses sensing technology to stay on your property and to avoid obstacles like trees, flower gardens and even the family dog. When its battery starts to run down, the AutoMower simply finds its docking station and recharges itself.

29. It is expected to sell at a price of $1,500 to $1,800.

30. Joseph Engelberger, chairman of Help-Mate Robotics in Danbury, Conn., says a multifunction home robot is a natural assistant for the aging population.

31. "It would be a companion for the elderly or infirm so they don't have to go to the nursing home," Engelberger said.

32. "It's a creature that would know the house, cook and clean, help you get out of bed, help you eat, monitor home security, or measure vital signs."

33. HelpMate, which already has more than seventy robots operating in hospitals throughout the United States is seeking to raise $5 million for the development of such a household robot.

34. The final product might be expensive. (At $50,000, Engelberger compares it to the cost of a luxury car.) But that same robot might lease for $600 or $700 a month —just a fraction of the cost of nursing-home care, or even of a daily visiting nurse.

35. "The economics are very powerful," Engelberger said.

36. But it is those same economics that are keeping the latest advances in robotics bottled up in laboratories, said Nejat Olgac, an engineering professor and robotics researcher at the University of Connecticut.

37. "I don't see a very urgent demand from the user side in improving robotic structures," Olgac said. "The folks who are doing research are basically crying out that they are not able to find users of what they can produce in their laboratories."

38. Until that "pull" from the demand site materializes, Olgac said, he believes robotics will remain largely the domain of researchers and hobbyists.

39. But others, like Moravec, say the demand is simply waiting for the right product at the right price.

FINDING THE MAIN IDEAS: CHUNKING

■ **READING TIP:**
Chunking means putting together all the paragraphs that deal with the same main idea. It is very useful especially when a reading is made up of very short paragraphs.

Rewrite the following main ideas according to the order in which they appear in the article. Decide on which paragraph(s) correspond to each main idea.

	MAIN IDEAS	*PARAGRAPHS*
Introduction	*Introduction*	*1–4*
Examples of self-guided machines	_____	_____
The money aspect	_____	_____
Previous robots	_____	_____
Three generations of robots	_____	_____
Recent advances	_____	_____
Robots and the elderly	_____	_____

Compare your list with a partner.

GETTING THE IMPORTANT INFORMATION

Complete the following statements in order to check how much information you were able to get. Do *not* look back at the article.

1. Robots will become commercially available in _____

   _____ years.

2. The problem with older robots was _____

   _____.

3. Robots should have the ability to _____

   _____ in order to function in the real world.

4. That skill is now possible because _____

   _____.

5. _____ generations of robots are expected in the next decade.

6. Cye and the Automower are examples of _____
   _____.

7. The age group that could benefit a lot from home robots is
   _____.

8. Home robots are not in high demand because _____
   _____.

Compare your answers with a partner. Then look back at the reading together to check your information.

REACTING TO THE INFORMATION

Discuss these questions with a partner or in a small group. Explain your answers.

1. Why do you think the dog AIBO, made by Sony, sold out so fast?
2. Which of the three robots—Cye, Automower, or AIBO—would you be most interested in?
3. Is there a need for robots that are capable of "feeling"? Why or why not?

EVALUATING THE INFORMATION

Scientists at Massachusetts Institute of Technology (MIT) are now working on designing a robot capable of feeling.

PREVIEWING

Read the title and subtitle. Discuss the following questions with a partner.

1. What could this robot look like?
2. What different emotions might it exhibit?
3. How should it be treated?

The Robot that Loves People

By Douglas Whynott

Machines that walk, talk, move, and show human-like emotions are no longer science fiction.

1. Walk by Cynthia Breazeal's workbench in MIT's Artificial Intelligence Lab, and you can't help but notice a hunk of aluminum filled with silicon chips and electric motors, a machine shaped and sized like a human head. Actually, what you notice is that it looks lonely. Its big, red rubber lips are turned down in a frown, its fuzzy eyebrows are heavy, its curly pink ears are drooping. Its huge baby-doll eyes are scanning the room, searching for someone.

2. So it's no wonder that when Breazeal comes into the room and sits down in front of her needy little robot, which she calls Kismet, its mood begins to change. Looking straight into Kismet's eyes, Breazeal offers a "human face stimulus." Kismet's eyebrows go straight up, making its baby blue eyes appear even wider as it looks straight back at its creator with growing interest. Then Kismet wiggles its ears up and down. "Greeting behavior," says Breazeal. Kismet's expressions alter into another state, the sort a parent loves to evoke in a child. Happiness. Kismet is all smiles. Breazeal, who created this creature, is not surprised. Next she talks baby

talk, cooing like a new mother. That keeps Kismet interested, smiling and watching. Just for contrast, Breazeal begins to move back and forth. Uh oh. Kismet doesn't like that at all. It looks annoyed, says Breazeal, because it's "over stimulated." Kismet turns up a lip, raises one eyebrow, lowers the other. The message is clear: Stop this nonsense! So Breazeal turns away, and Kismet grows calmer, but only for a while. Deprived of attention, face stimulus gone, Kismet grows sad. Brazeal turns around. Happiness returns. Breazeal can keep this going, keep Kismet happy by paying constant attention to the robot as if it were an infant, which in a sense it is. She can, for example, pick up a toy stuffed dinosaur and begin playing with Kismet. Kismet likes that. But like an infant, Kismet can become tired. Enough of this, Kismet seems to say, as it slowly closes its eyes and goes to sleep.

3. Cynthia Breazeal, the daughter of a mathematician and a computer scientist, had grown up watching *Star Wars* and *Star Trek*. When she arrived at MIT in 1990 to begin working on her master's degree in electrical engineering and computer science, she didn't have a specific project in mind, only a general vision. She knew she wanted to build a robot. At first she was fascinated by the robots being built by Rodney Brooks, an MIT professor and innovator in artificial intelligence. At the time, Brooks was working on a big project: an android (human-like robot) inspired by Commander Data in the *Star Trek* television series. Cog, the android, could make eye contact and move its head to track a moving object. Then Cog could move like a human. Its formidable but gentle arms could throw and catch a ball, play with a Slinky, point at things, even listen to rock 'n' roll and beat out a corresponding rhythm on a drum.

4. Meanwhile, Breazeal began studying the process of cognitive development in children. "I began to get interested in the idea that infants are the simplest people. I wanted people to be able to naturally treat the robot as if it were an infant, to naturally help the robot as much as they could." And she began to think that she needed something different from Cog. "You look at Cog and you realize that no one is going to treat Cog like an infant," she says with a laugh. "It's this huge six-foot-five robot. Its face is way up there, you can't get close to it, and it has no facial expressions. So I started thinking about building a separate robot that focused on communication abilities that I cared about. I wanted to have face-to-face exchange, with expressions and eventually vocalization. And that's when I started building Kismet, in the summer of 1997." Breazeal took a spare Cog head and reengineered it, lengthening the

neck, adding a jaw. She got the eyes from a special-effects supplier in Los Angeles. He told her to make them big and blue, like the Gerber baby, if she wanted people to treat her robot like an infant. He also helped her place a color camera into the pupil of each eye. She set up small motors to move facial features—eyebrows that lift and arch, ears that lift and rotate, jaws that open and close, and lips that bend, straighten, and curl.

5. Breazeal also had to write special software consisting of what she calls "drives" and "emotions." Drives are similar to needs, and there are three in Kismet. The social drive becomes a need for people, the stimulation drive seeks toys and other objects, and the fatigue drive creates a need for sleep. Each drive has a normal position it wants to be in. When ignored, the drives move into an under-stimulated regime, so needs grow for social interaction and stimulation. Too much activity and the drives drift into the over-stimulated regime, and a need grows for a break from the action. Happiness, interest, and calm are near the normal position. Outside that area lie other responses: sadness, boredom, fear, disgust, and anger. Depending on information flowing in through Kismet's eyes and the state of its motivational system, strategies form that activate behavior.

6. Inspired by her study of the relationship between a mother and her infant, Breazeal wanted to create a powerful social manipulator. Just as a baby uses expressions, kicks, and cries to manipulate the mother into satisfying its needs and desires, Kismet is designed to engage people in a wide variety of social interactions that satisfy its internal drives. Because the nature of Kismet is ultimately to learn, to become more sophisticated, and to develop as a social creature, it is driven to engage people and to keep them engaged.

7. As Kismet begins to learn, Breazeal says, it will slowly become more socially sophisticated, like an infant becoming a small child. That will bring Breazeal a lot closer to achieving her real goal. "To me," she says without hesitation, "the ultimate milestone is a robot that can be your friend. To me, that's the ultimate in social intelligence."

8. Breazeal says her work is still research, "so much at the beginning that we haven't even begun yet." But it is the first step to a future that Breazeal and Brooks deeply believe in, a future they both want. At some point robots and humans will coexist, Breazeal says. And they won't just be appliances; they'll be friends. Brooks says developing androids challenges humans' "last refuge of specialness." At first we thought the Earth was the center of the universe. And then there was Darwin. And then Crick and Watson showed that we're all made from the same DNA, essentially. And they said that a computer couldn't play chess, and when a computer could play chess, they said it couldn't feel. We're trying to push on that boundary. That's all that's sort of left to us, all there is to be special about. And so we're trying to see if we can make a machine that has emotions. We don't know exactly how to do it, but we're trying to do it." And if they're successful, will it be a person? "How will we know?" she answers.

SCANNING: TRACING THE DEVELOPMENT OF AN IDEA

Read through the article quickly and outline the steps that led to the development of Kismet.

- Cynthia Breazeal grows up watching *Star Wars* and *Star Trek*.

- _____

- _____

- _____

- _____

NOTE-TAKING: FINDING EVIDENCE

Read the article quickly and find support for the following:

■ Kismet's human-like appearance

_____

_____

_____

_____

■ Kismet's baby-like behavior

_____

_____

_____

_____

_____

_____

■ Breazeal's mother-like behavior

_____

_____

_____

_____

_____

Work with a partner. Use the brief notes you made to talk about the article. Discuss the following.

1. Do you feel that Kismet is on the way to becoming 'human-like' in its actions?
2. Why are scientists interested in designing a robot like that?
3. Would you like to own Kismet? Why or why not?

After Reading

GIVING YOUR OPINION

Several controversial ideas/issues have been raised in these articles. Two of them are listed below. Look back at the readings and find two more.

1. Having a robot look after you is better than going to a nursing home.

2. Human beings are becoming less and less special.

3. _____

4. _____

Discuss these ideas with a partner or in a small group. Be ready to explain your opinion.

EXPLORING THE CONSEQUENCES

The following predictions have been made about robots. Discuss what the consequences could be if these predictions came true.

1. "Robots will evolve in simple steps just like humans did—but 10 million times faster. They will surpass human intelligence in the next 50 years."
2. "At some point robots and humans will coexist. And they won't just be appliances; they'll be friends."

Vocabulary Building

REFERENCE WORDS

Words like *this, that, these, those,* and *such* are used in order to avoid repeating an idea and to provide continuity in reading or writing. The following words/phrases are taken from the first reading, "Even Sony's Betting on a Robotic Future," and are listed in the order in which they appear. Locate each word/phrase and note what it is referring to. The first one has been done as an example.

1. such things were possible

   mechanical creatures that looked like humans and could think.

2. that kind of robot

   _____

3. those creatures

   _____

4. this news

   _____

5. these are people

   _____

EXPRESSIONS IN CONTEXT

English, like many other languages, has some common expressions that are best understood when read in context. Use the following contexts to find the meaning of the *boldface* expressions. Explain each in your own words.

1. Years ago when science-fiction novels were an obsession with most boys and girls, **the robot was king**.

   _____

2. Then **the wind shifted** and robots were no longer popular.

   _____

3. The importance of this news isn't that some company thinks it **can turn a buck** selling robots.

   _____

4. Robots have started doing all kinds of things. Their performance is **astronomically above** what it was in the seventies and eighties when they could just about move across a room.

   _____

5. **The ultimate milestone** for Cynthia Breazeal is a robot that can be your friend.

_____

6. Rapid advances in technology have allowed researchers to build machines that are capable of **thinking on their feet**.

_____

Check your answers with a partner or with your teacher. Practice using these expressions by putting each into a sentence of your own.

1. _____

2. _____

3. _____

4. _____

5. _____

6. _____

Expanding Your Language

SPEAKING

A. Debate: Some people feel that the world is already overpopulated and therefore we should not be spending money on making human-like machines. Do you agree or disagree with this opinion? Work with a partner who has the same position. Together, think of and present reasons supporting your position. Prepare to talk for two to three minutes about your ideas. Practice explaining your point of view with your partner. When you are ready, present your point of view to someone who has a different argument.

B. Talk It Out: Work with a partner or with a small group of students. Discuss if being a woman made a difference in the kind of robot Cynthia Breazeal built. Find out what people think about typical male and female jobs. Find out if it is common for women to have jobs similar to Cynthia Breazeal's.

WRITING

A. **Reaction Writing:** In "Exploring the Consequences" (p. 153) you discussed two predictions. Write your reaction to the following questions:
1. Do you think these predictions will come true?
2. Should we allow them to come true?
3. Would you like to live in a world in which all your needs were supplied by human-like robots?

B. **Personal Writing:** Write about a goal that you had as a child or teenager. Include information about where the idea for that goal came from, whether it was easy/hard to achieve or whether you are still in the process of achieving it.

The Internet—How Do We Deal with It?

Chapter Openers

QUESTIONNAIRE

Think about your use of the Internet and complete the following questionnaire in note form.

1. How often do you use the Internet?

2. What do you use it for?

_____

3. Do you do any shopping on the Internet? If yes, check (✔) the items that you shop for. Add a few items of your own.

_____ Food/household items

_____ Clothes

_____ Books

_____ CDs, videos, DVDs

_____ Sporting equipment

_____ Furniture

_____ Computer software

_____

_____

4. What advice do you have for people who want to shop online?

_____

_____

Share what you wrote with a partner or with a small group. Discuss any problems that you have had with the Internet.

MATCHING

Every field has expressions that are specific to it. The area of computers is no different. Column A consists of terms that are now often associated with computers. Match these terms with the correct definition from Column B.

Column A	Column B
_____ 1. on-line	a. to go from one site to another on the Internet
_____ 2. link	b. connected to or controlled by a computer

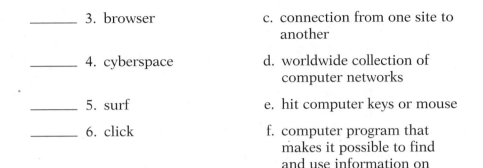

_____ 3. browser

c. connection from one site to another

_____ 4. cyberspace

d. worldwide collection of computer networks

_____ 5. surf

e. hit computer keys or mouse

_____ 6. click

f. computer program that makes it possible to find and use information on the Internet

Check your answers with a partner. Ask your teacher to clarify any words you do not understand.

Exploring and Understanding Reading

PREDICTING

Circle *A* if you agree or *D* if you disagree with the statement.

1. A D The Internet is changing the way we deal with one another.

2. A D Online shopping is the fastest-growing Internet sector.

3. A D The Internet will never become as popular as television.

4. A D The Internet is an inexpensive way of having a good time.

Compare your answers with a partner. You do not have to agree, but explain your opinions as completely as possible. After you finish reading, return to these questions and answer them based on the information you read.

SKIMMING

Read the article quickly and choose the statement that best expresses the general idea of the reading.

a. Internet shopping is becoming very popular.

b. The Internet is developing very fast and is changing many of the ways we do things.

c. The Internet will soon become a major source of entertainment.

Leave It to Browser

1. No longer just a place where misfits go to hack or teenagers go to chat, the Internet has quickly become a significant cultural force that influences the economy and absorbs our free time. Over the past five years, the Net's phenomenal growth has forever altered the way many people keep in touch with distant friends, buy airline tickets, get news and sports scores, invest in stocks, do research at the office, or look for a job.

2. A recent survey of 4,350 Americans with Internet connections at home—by Greenfield Online, a market research firm in Westport, Connecticut—paints a fascinating picture of how the information age is changing daily routines. More than 70 percent of those surveyed log on several times a week just after getting home from work, and a quarter of those stay online all evening. And Web surfing is even taking over the sacred American tradition, watching television: half of all those surveyed say that they now watch less, and 19 percent declare that the Internet is more important to them than TV.

3. On-line shopping is the fastest-growing Internet sector. Investors have shown amazing confidence in the Web economy, sending the stocks of companies like Amazon.com and iVillage very high despite the fact that not one has turned a profit. Products that don't have to be touched or tried on—like books, CDs, or software—remain the most popular online purchases. But consumers are also saving trips to the mall by buying more clothes, jewelry, and even home furnishings via the Internet.

4. Perhaps the surest sign of consumer willingness to shop online is the runaway popularity of eBay—the largest and most successful auction site on the Web, drawing more than ten million visitors per month. EBay's thousands of vendors sell just about anything—from computers to opera tickets to used postcards—and buyers continue to bid on pretty much all of it.

5. While e-commerce thrives, the Internet remains one of the few places where you don't have to spend a lot to have a good time. A rapidly increasing number of Americans—not just kids—play games on the Net. With processor and Internet-connection speeds doubling every couple of years, the boundaries for games are quickly disappearing, and the new millennium could see an explosion in this market.

6. Even surfing the Web for news or weather reports is somehow more enjoyable—more like a game—than turning the pages of a newspaper or a magazine. The fact that networked Americans now rely on the Internet for news more than newspapers or the radio can't just be due to convenience. There is a certain freedom in the hugeness of the Web that makes even boring tasks seem new and, well, pretty cool.

—Fortune

RECOGNIZING MAIN IDEAS AND DETAILS

■ READING TIP:
Recognizing the difference between more general information (main points) and details is an important critical reading skill.

The author states several important ideas and provides details to support these points. Circle *M* if the statement is a main point and *D* if it is a detail.

1. M   D   The wired age is changing daily routines.

2. M   D   On-line shopping is the fastest growing Internet sector.

3. M   D   More than 70% log on several times a week just after getting home from work.

4. M   D   You can have a good time on the Internet.

5. M   D   Stocks of companies like Amazon.com and iVillage are soaring.

6. M   D   A rapidly increasing number of Americans play games on the Net.

7. M   D   19% declare that the Internet is more important to them than watching television.

8. M   D   The Internet is affecting television.

List the main points on one side and the corresponding details on the other side.

MAIN POINT   DETAIL

1. _____   _____

   _____   _____

2. _____   _____

3. _____   _____

Check your answers with a partner.

USING GRAPHIC INFORMATION

On-line shopping is the fastest growing Internet sector. The following are some graphs and tables that show the present situation as well as future projections. Use the information presented to answer the questions that follow.

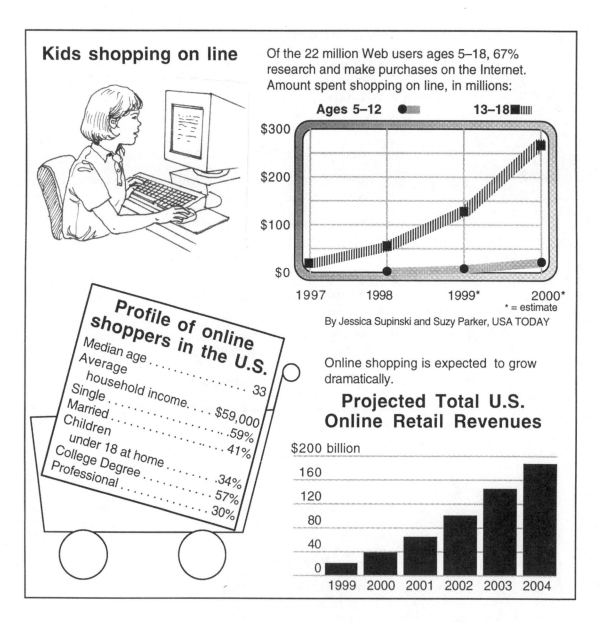

Kids shopping on line

Of the 22 million Web users ages 5–18, 67% research and make purchases on the Internet. Amount spent shopping on line, in millions:

Ages 5–12 ●   **13–18** ▦

* = estimate

By Jessica Supinski and Suzy Parker, USA TODAY

Profile of online shoppers in the U.S.

Median age 33
Average household income. $59,000
Single 59%
Married 41%
Children under 18 at home 34%
College Degree 57%
Professional 30%

Online shopping is expected to grow dramatically.

Projected Total U.S. Online Retail Revenues

$200 billion

1. How much did Web users aged thirteen to eighteen spend in 1999? In 2000?
   Why could that be a problem?
   How do you think they are paying? With their own credit cards? With parents' credit cards?

2. How much are the revenues expected to increase between 1999 and 2000? How much are they expected to increase between 2003 and 2004?

3. Who is more likely to shop online: single people or married people? Why?

Check your answers with a partner. Make sure you support your ideas with explanations or reasons.

PAIRED READINGS

The two readings that follow are about different aspects of Internet shopping. One is about the extremely successful auction site, eBay, and the other is about young people aged five through eighteen shopping online. Choose one of the articles and work with a partner who is reading the *same* article.

Reading 1: Auction Nation

PREDICTING

Read the title and the subtitle of Reading 1 and answer the following questions.

- What are the functions and characteristics of a community center?

  _____

  _____

  _____

- In what ways can an Internet auction site resemble a community center?

  _____

  _____

  _____

Discuss your answers with your partner.

SURVEYING/CHUNKING

▪ **READING TIP:**
When surveying, it is useful to read the last sentence as well as the first sentence of every paragraph because it sometimes states the idea of the paragraph more clearly.

Read the introduction (paragraphs 1 and 2) and the first and last sentence of every paragraph after that. You will find that there are six main ideas in addition to the introduction and conclusion. Some of these ideas have been entered in the following list. Fill in the remaining main ideas as well the paragraphs corresponding to each main idea.

Main Idea	Paragraph
Introduction (Melissa Wicker)	*1, 2*
How eBay similar to community	_____
_____	*4, 5*
Antique dealers	_____
_____	_____
How eBay leads to sociability	_____
_____	*9, 10*
Conclusion	*11*

Check your main ideas with a partner. Quickly scan the article together to confirm or change what you have.

Auction Nation

By Andrew Ferguson

Town square, community center, social scene— eBay turned into much more than an auction.

1. Melissa Wicker likes to shop for her friends. And she has a lot of friends— nearly 8 million, at last count. Of course, the word friend is used loosely these days, in an era when e-mail establishes instant intimacy between total strangers separated by thousands of miles. So it's no surprise that Wicker, 46, an assistant district attorney in Isle of Palms, South Carolina, hasn't met many of her new friends in the flesh. But they're on her mind when she visits clothing stores and comes upon an interesting discount in designer duds. She buys by the armful, goes home to her computer and within a couple of days has set up her own fashion show—on eBay, in full view of anyone with a modem and a yen to bid on the clothes she puts up for auction. Bids race through cyberspace, winners are declared, and Wicker mails the goods to the lucky buyers—and cashes their money orders and cashier's checks, sometimes for a tidy profit and always with the thrill of a successful sale. "I've been waiting for eBay my whole life," she says.

2. And she has lots of company, among buyers and sellers alike. EBay makes a lot of people happy, and not just because it makes some people rich. The surprise— you might even call it the miracle—of eBay is that it offers online consumers something rarer, more essential, more enduring than a chance to make a profit. It offers them a sense of community.

3. For many people, eBay does what communities have traditionally done. It not only provides them with financial support but also draws them together with like-minded folk, offering encouragement, rewarding unique talents and interests, giving an outlet for their eccentricities and individuality and in some cases rescuing them from situations where they would otherwise suffer alone.

4. Consider Carol Sangster of Edmonton, Canada, who seven years ago had to quit her job as an engineering clerk at Canadian National Railways because she was struggling with systemic lupus and diabetes. For several years, she fought for her life. In time she partially recovered. "I became well enough to be bored," she says. Then, 18 months ago, she discovered eBay.

5. In their travels over the years, she and her husband had acquired acres of stuff. She started putting lots of it up for auction. When she was well enough, she began attending public auctions and buying up a lot. Today she tests her strength, challenging herself with eBay, working as much as her illness allows. "For me," she says, "it wasn't the sale, it was being part of something again. It was the contact with people. I guess I used it to make me feel better."

6. Many antiques dealers, who would seem most threatened by eBay, have seen their livelihoods transformed. David James, for example, opened his shop in Alexandria, Virginia, eight years ago. He deals mostly in what the trade calls smalls: candlesticks, glassware and other such collectibles. He's still got the store, but today his business—and his life—revolve around a warehouse a few miles away, where he stores the treasures he has collected. From a crowded, windowless room, he monitors the hundreds of auctions he has posted—moving anywhere from $40,000 to $75,000 a month. He has hired a full-time employee to oversee his eBay business and plans to move to a new space complete with a miniprocessing center.

7. For as long as there has been an Internet, of course, there have been anti-Internet people who claim that this will be the end of face-to-face sociability as people retreat from the public square to their computers for the anonymous encounters of cyberspace. With some justification, the pessimists can trace the decline of shopping, that most social of activities, from the mom-and-pop corner shop, where everyone knows everyone, to the department store, where we might recognize one of the cashiers, and from there to the vast warehouse of the superstore, where no one knows anyone—and finally to the Internet, where human contact is reduced to electrons.

8. But the evidence suggests that eBay represents a return to that earlier one-on-one sociability—and maybe even improves on it, since the Net collapses the traditional divisions of geography and class. Wherever you plant your modem, the new economy arrives. Take Patricia Hoyt, who lives in Baker, Montana, roughly 225 miles from the nearest big city, Billings. The old economy of oil and cattle has not been kind to Baker, and when oil prices dropped, business dried up at the motel Hoyt and her husband own.

9. But Hoyt had a hobby: making decorative glass beads. Thanks to eBay, her hobby is now her livelihood. She sells as many as 3,000 beads a month, for as much as $50 each. EBay has given her more than a new career. She refers without irony to the bead community she has discovered online. Glass beads have created an entire network of chat groups and e-mail lists. Many of her customers buy weekly. "If I don't put up any auctions for a week," she says, "they'll write me and ask, 'Are you OK?'"

10. Before complaining about the breaking up of American society by eBay and the Internet at large, the worrywarts should talk to Mary Ellen and Don Millbranth. Last year they were strangers, both widowed. Don, 66, a retired engineer, in Wanatah, Indiana, decided to sell a paperback book about miniature cabinets, his new hobby, on eBay. Mary Ellen, 61, bought it for $7.10 (including shipping). One thing led to another, as tends to happen on the Internet. After a particularly passionate weekend of e-mail (more than 200 in 48 hours, by Mary Ellen's count), they decided to meet in Mary Ellen's hometown of Huntsville, Alabama. It was, needless to say, Valentine's Day. They were married three months later.

11. The Millbranths may be an extreme example of eBay's social benefits. But it is these examples that show that the eBay phenomenon is a sign of a fundamentally healthy society. The sociologist James Coleman coined the term "social capital" to describe the shared values and habits that allow individuals to cooperate for a common purpose. Without it, societies collapse. Trust is the essential element of social capital, and eBay cannot operate without the assumption that your buyer or seller is basically a decent sort. Fraud on eBay is remarkably rare: eBay's figures show fewer than 1 percent of transactions have involved fraud. This suggests that eBayers are trustworthy. Chris Spencer, a show-business manager in Southern California who lists as many as 3,000 items monthly, says eBay confirms for him the essential goodness of human nature. "The average person is honest and decent," he says. "That's what eBay is about—honesty. I have cashed thousands of checks and have had just one bounce."

–Time

USING MAIN IDEAS TO SCAN FOR DETAILS

Read the questions and using your list of main ideas decide which paragraph contains the relevant information. Scan the paragraph to find the answer. Write the answer in note form as well as the number of the paragraph where you found the information.

1. How does Melissa Wicker get paid for what she sells?

   _____

2. Name three important things that eBay provides for people.

   _____

   _____

   _____

3. a. Where did Carol Sangster get her stuff?

   _____

   b. What is she getting from eBay?

   _____

4. a. According to the anti-Internet people, what was the earliest form of modern shopping?

   _____

   b. What is the latest form? (not including the Internet)

   _____

5. a. Why did Patricia Hoyts begin a new business in the Internet?

   _____

   b. How much a month can she make now?

   _____

6. What does the eBay phenomenon say about society in general?

   _____

Check your answers with a partner. Refer to the reading if you do not agree.

RECAPPING THE INFORMATION: HIGHLIGHTING

A. Highlight information that relates to these ideas:

1. Criticisms of the Internet
2. Examples of the social benefits of eBay.

B. Compare what you highlighted with your partner. Discuss whether you highlighted too much or too little. Add any highlighting you need to.

C. Using *only* what you highlighted, take turns telling each other the important information in the article. Make sure you explain the information and check to see that your partner has understood.

REACTING TO THE INFORMATION

Discuss these questions with a partner.

1. Why is eBay so important to Patricia Hoyt?
2. Does it surprise you to find that people are so honest when using eBay? How would you explain this?
3. Do you think you can become "friends" with a person you have never met face-to face?

■ ■
_____

Reading 2: There's a Mall in My Bedroom

PREDICTING

Read the title and the subtitle of Reading 2 and answer the following questions.

■ What are some ways that kids can be taught how to handle money?

_____

_____

■ How can online shopping do the same thing?

Discuss your answers with your partner.

SURVEYING/CHUNKING

■ *READING TIP:*
See page 164.

Read the introduction (paragraphs 1 and 2) and the first and last sentence of every paragraph after that. You will find that there are six main ideas in addition to the introduction and conclusion. Some of these ideas have been entered in the following list. Fill in the remaining main ideas as well the paragraphs corresponding to each main idea.

Main Idea	Paragraph
Introduction (sites for kids)	*1, 2*
Why kids like site	
	4
How to save	
	8
General money management	*7, 9*
Restrictions	
Conclusion	*12*

Check your main ideas with a partner. Quickly scan the article together to confirm or change what you have.

There's a Mall in My Bedroom

By Mindy Charski

New Web sites promise to teach kids about money while they shop

1. It's not that Tracey Baker, 18, doesn't like the mall anymore. It's just that it's so easy to buy CDs, T-shirts, Beanie Babies, and books from the confines of her Carmel Valley, California, home on a new Web site called RocketCash.com. Dad deposits $100 a month in her RocketCash account, and she can spend it at any of 50 affiliated merchants without having to nag him for his credit-card number.

2. Children between 5 and 18 years old will spend an estimated $1.3 billion online by 2002, predicts Jupiter Communications, the Internet research firm. Three different sites all went online this year to look for young e-shoppers. More will surely follow—but is that good or bad news for parents who want their kids to learn the value of a dollar? So far, the answer is mixed.

3. It's easy to understand why kids like the sites. Mom and Dad deposit a sum in the child's name. The child is free to spend until it's gone, linking to such online vendors as CDNow and Delias, whose clothes are adored by teenage girls. At one site, relatives can give gift certificates. Another site lets children create birthday or Christmas wish lists. The Web sites take about 5 percent of

each purchase price, but there's no markup: The consumer pays the price posted on the Web site.

4. Give and get. But it's not just about making money, or so the sites say. Two of the sites encourage kids to donate money to charity online. "Ex-Spice Girl Geri Halliwell is a big fan of supporting charity," proclaims one of these sites. "And now she's got a gift for you with ANY donation of $1 or more to ANY iCanBuy charity!"

5. Two of the three sites advise kids how to save as well as spend. "Our research showed teens really wanted the freedom of acting like adults but were insecure about their financial strength and wanted guidance," says Ginger Thomson, the president of one of these sites. Her site posts articles in teen speak on topics like saving up for a prom date or finding a mutual fund that's good for kids, and also has games to help teens learn to spend wisely. One site provides links to educational financial sites.

6. Young people can even watch their money grow. Two sites offer on-line bank accounts. Through iCanBuy's affiliate, the online bank Security First Net-work Bank, kids can keep their money in a checking account with an impressive 5.83 percent interest rate. Kids can't yet transfer money to their iCanBuy spending account, but they can at another site, which offers a savings account with a 3.2 percent interest rate. "You know where your money is all the time," says 13-year-old Ellen Dahlke of Evergreen Park, Illinois, who deposits earnings from babysitting as well as her allowance.

7. RocketCash's philosophy is that teens are not interested in lessons, says cofounder Carol Kruse. She believes they will learn money management by comparison shopping on the site.

8. Or perhaps they'll just learn new ways to spend it. "These sites cover their selling to kids under the financial responsibility mantle," says Kathryn Montgomery, president of the consumer group Center for Media Education. "I find that argument hard to buy." She worries that the intense marketing could lead to "incredible exploitation," pushing kids into impulse buying.

9. Shipping news. True, the sites do stress spending, acknowledges Dara Duguay, executive director of Jumpstart —a nonprofit organization that encourages financial literacy for children—but they also teach about money. Financial ignorance is so high among kids that any venue to start a conversation about money is valuable, she believes. A 1999 study found that only 29 percent of students say they get "a lot" of parental guidance about money. Other experts say kids have to learn the ways of e-commerce sooner or later. One lesson: Buying a group of items at once keeps down shipping costs.

10. To reassure parents, the sites let Mom and Dad see a list of what their child bought and restrict the merchants their children can visit. Two sites let parents put a ceiling on individual purchases. The third site allows them to select the hours that their kids are allowed to shop online.

11. The sites themselves set some limits, too. One site promises to preselect items from its vendors that seem suitable for the 7-to-17 age group that it courts. The other two sites, which are primarily for teenagers, censor x-rated books and videos.

12. What does this all mean? It means that parents can't take anything for granted when it comes to the Web. Until recently, one site let youngsters buy a CD recording with a sexually explicit song. After a *U.S. News* reporter asked about that CD, the cofounder Paul Herman took it off the list.

–U.S. News & World Report

USING MAIN IDEAS TO SCAN FOR DETAILS

Read the questions and use your list of main ideas to decide which paragraph contains the relevant information. Scan the paragraph to find the answer. Write the answer in note form.

1. a. How much can Tracey Baker spend every month?

   _____

   b. How much will kids be spending by the year 2002?

   _____

2. Name two ways that Ginger Thomson uses to show kids how to save money.

   _____

   _____

3. According to Katherine Montgomery, what do these sites encourage kids to do?

   _____

4. What percentage of students get financial advice from their parents?

   _____

5. Name two ways parents can monitor their kids' shopping.

   _____

   _____

6. How do different sites restrict what kids can buy?

   _____

Check your answers with a partner. Refer to the reading if you do not agree.

RECAPPING THE INFORMATION: HIGHLIGHTING

A. Highlight information that relates to these ideas:

1. Description of sites
2. What sites can teach children
3. Criticism of sites

B. Compare what you highlighted with your partner. Discuss whether you highlighted too much or too little. Add any highlighting you need to.

C. Using *only* what you highlighted, take turns telling each other the important information in the article. Make sure you explain the information and check to see that your partner has understood.

REACTING TO THE INFORMATION

1. Are these kids really learning the value of money? Support your answer.
2. How does the establishment of such sites encourage impulse buying?
3. Are the restrictions adequate enough to control what the kids buy?

After Reading

RETELLING THE INFORMATION

Work with a partner who read a different article. Use what you highlighted to retell the information. Explain the ideas clearly in your own words. Encourage your partner to ask questions about the information or write some of the important facts you explain. After you have finished retelling, discuss the questions in "Reacting to the Information."

REACTING TO THE READINGS

Work with a partner or with a small group. Using all the readings and your own ideas and experiences, answer the following questions.

1. What are the advantages of buying and selling on the Internet?
2. Is it a good idea to be able "to get what we want whenever we want it"?
3. What are some of the problems that can occur?
4. In what ways is the Internet changing our lives and our relationships?

APPLYING THE INFORMATION: CONTRASTING IDEAS

The people mentioned in the readings so far feel quite positive about using the Internet. Read the following article to get a different point of view. Answer these questions.

- What was the author looking for?
- Did she find it through the Web?

Holiday Headache

By Anita Hamilton

Was it really too much, asking the Web to help me find a New Years getaway? Apparently so.

All I wanted was a log cabin in Maine, somewhere deep in the woods, to toast the New Year under the stars. It was to be my first vacation with my boyfriend, and I wanted it to be perfect. So rather than waste money on a guidebook that was bound to be outdated before it hit the shelves, I decided to search online. Little did I know that when I typed the words; Maine log cabin rental at altavista. com, I was stepping into 48 hours of Internet hell.

Forget dinner, forget work, forget sleep. I was glued to my computer for hours as I obsessively searched the Web. When I found my first mega Web site dedicated to vacation rentals, I happily clicked from one listing to another, certain I would quickly find the perfect hideaway.

I was wrong. The first site that I tried, grouped rentals by region but had no map to tell me where such romantic-sounding places as Seal Cove or Owl's Head were. So I had to log on to another site to locate each one, then return to slogging through listings. My computer was choking under the strain. Another site, let me zero in on cabins and cottages. I got fifty matches right off, but most of the rentals turned out to be closed for the winter—something I learned only after reading a lot of fine print. I tried branching out and found a "millennium special" in Tennessee's Smoky Mountains. But at $1,300 for a long weekend, it sounded to me more like a millennium rip-off.

One day and hundreds of listings later, I was ready to throw my computer out the window. For every ten vacation spots I looked into, I found maybe one that sounded good—and more often than not it was booked, too far away, or outrageously priced. For all the hype about the Net making searches easier, it often gives you too many options and too few real choices. All it was giving me was a headache.

I finally decided to put our log-cabin Web dreams on hold and search the old-fashioned way—at a bookstore. I bought a paperback called America's Favorite Inns, B&Bs, and Small Hotels. I was relieved to see that each city was neatly pinpointed on a detailed map, and most had good descriptions to help me figure out where in Maine we should go in the first place. Even better, I could read the book in bed or on the subway. It was so civilized.

When I saw that the guide listed most B&Bs' Web sites at the top of each review, I almost cried. I knew I couldn't resist taking a peek, even though it meant dragging out my search that much longer as I dutifully read the printed reviews, then waited for each site to pop up onscreen.

Then I found it: an old inn on the southern coast of Maine that rented us one of its best rooms for $100 a night. Guess what? It didn't have a Web site. I took my chances based on a good review, a great location and a bargain price. It wasn't a log cabin, and it was miles from the woods, but there were lace curtains, a hardwood floor and a quilt on the bed. With the ocean outside our window and a fireplace in the room, my New Year's Eve was just as cozy as I dreamed it would be.

–Time

DISCUSSION QUESTIONS

Discuss the following questions with a partner or with a small group.

1. Why did the writer initially choose to use the Web instead of a guide book?
2. What different problems did she have at the different sites?
3. What were the advantages of using a guide book?
4. Discuss what she means by the statement "the Net . . . often gives you too many options and too few real choices."

▮ Vocabulary Building

EXPRESSIONS IN CONTEXT

Match each of the boldface expressions in the following sentences with one of the words listed below.

Column 1

———— 1. She buys **by the armful**.

———— 2. A market research firm in Westport, Connecticut **paints a** fascinating **picture** of how the information age is changing daily routines.

———— 3. EBay cannot operate without the assumption that the buyer or seller is basically **a decent sort**.

———— 4. "I find that argument **hard to buy**."

———— 5. Two sites let parents put a **ceiling** on individual purchases.

———— 6. Perhaps the surest sign of consumer willingness to shop online is the **runaway** popularity of eBay.

Column 2

a. a good person.   b. difficult to believe   c. describes

d. a lot   e. rapid rise in   f. limit

Check your answers with a partner.

VOCABULARY IN CONTEXT

Use the context to find the meaning of the words that have been underlined. Write the definition of each word.

1. The sociologist James Coleman <u>coined</u> the term "social capital" to describe the shared values and habits that allow individuals to cooperate for a common purpose.

———————————————————————

2. "I have cashed thousands of checks and have had just one <u>bounce</u>."

———————————————————————

3. <u>Fraud</u> on eBay is remarkably rare: eBay's figures show fewer than 1 percent of transactions have involved <u>fraud</u>. This suggests that eBayers are trustworthy.

4. She visits clothing stores and comes upon an interesting discount in designer <u>duds</u>.

5. She has set up her own show on eBay in full view of anyone with a <u>yen</u> to bid on the clothes she puts up for auction.

6. Financial ignorance is so high among kids that any <u>venue</u> to start a conversation about money is valuable.

Check your definitions with a partner. Refer to a dictionary if necessary.

Expanding Your Language

SPEAKING

A. Role Play: Work with a partner. Imagine that one of you has so far resisted subscribing to the Internet and that the other is a strong supporter of the Internet. Prepare some arguments that support your position. Have a dialogue in which each of you is trying to convince the other.

B. Oral Presentation: Work with a partner. Prepare five interview questions to find out how your family and friends feel about the Internet. Interview at least three people and report back to your partner in the following class.

WRITING

Reaction Writing: Write about whether the effect of the Internet on our lives is mostly positive or negative. Use the information in the chapter readings as well as any ideas of your own. Explore as much as you can.

Read On: Taking It Further

READING SUGGESTIONS

In many places we find articles discussing how the Internet is being abused; examples of abuse include deceptive advertising, addiction to on-line shopping, and criminal activity.

Check newspapers or newsmagazines over the next few days and find an example of such a story.

- Read the article.
- Select a few main points.
- Highlight the interesting/relevant information.
- Present the ideas from your article to a partner or to the class.

Attitude Matters

*An optimist is a fellow who believes
what's going to be, will be postponed.*

– Kim Hubbard

181

Emotions affect how we experience so much in our lives—our relationships, our achievements, even our health. In this unit, we will explore the workings of powerful emotions and find out if and how our emotions can be controlled and used in a positive way. Chapter 9 is about anger: what it is, what it brings, how we experience it, and how we can cope with it. Chapter 10 looks on the brighter side at our feelings of hope and optimism and how these attitudes affect our lives. Together, these chapters present a part of the complex nature of human emotions.

Points of Interest

Dr. Jekyll and Mr. Hyde **tells the story of one man who experienced extreme mood and personality changes. The story details frightening effects that this condition has on his life and the lives of his friends and family. How do emotions, both positive and negative, affect our lives?**

CHAPTER 9

Anger: How to Use It

Chapter Openers

EXPRESSIONS

Here are some sayings about anger. Read and ask yourself what the writer wants us to understand about the power of anger. Is anger a productive or a destructive force? Is anger something we control or does it control us?

1. Never go to bed angry.

2. Never try to pacify people at the time of their rage.

3. A just man is slow to anger and quick to forgive.

4. Anger robs a person of wisdom.

5. Anger is seldom without a reason, but seldom a good one.

6. It is easy to be angry. But to be angry with the right person, to the right degree, at the right time, for the right purpose, and in the right way—this is not easy.

7. Anger is the only thing to put off 'til tomorrow.

8. I don't get mad, I get even.

What sayings about anger do you know? Think of one to share with your classmates.

DISCUSSION QUESTIONS

Discuss the following questions with a partner or in a small group.

1. Have you ever been angry? Can anger harm your health?

2. Can people stop themselves from being angry? What are some ways to do this?

3. Do people get angrier today than in the past? If so, why?

PAIRED READINGS

Choose Reading 1, which follows, or Reading 2, which is found in the Exercise section on pages E–4 and E–5. Quickly read the article, and based on the information, decide if the writer is suggesting that anger harms your health or not. Work with a partner who is reading the *same* article and discuss your opinion.

Reading 1: How Ideas Affect Us

Hotheads and Heart Attacks

If there's still another sequel to *Grumpy Old Men,* an appropriate place to film it might be a coronary care unit. So suggests the heart journal *Circulation,* which last week reported a study in which researchers tested 1,305 healthy men ages 40 to 90 for their ability to control anger and then followed them for seven years to see who had heart attacks. Conclusion: In the grumpiest men, the guys who often feel like swearing and smashing things, anger more than tripled the risk of nonfatal heart attacks and fatal coronary heart disease, even after adjusting for smoking and drinking.

"Anger releases stress hormones like adrenalin, which increases the stickiness of the blood and can cause clotting in the coronary arteries and heart attack," explains the study's author, Ichiro Kawachi, an assistant professor at the Harvard School of Public Health. "The more often they are angry, the more they are at risk." Fortunately, the study also found evidence that even in the chronically grumpy, a daily aspirin lowered the heart disease risk, though only a moderate 15 percent. Kawachi also suggests stress-reduction strategies like meditation. And, better yet, "avoid situations that give rise to anger."

– *U.S. News & World Report*

RECAPPING THE INFORMATION

■ READING TIP:
Remember that most reports of studies include the type of study, the author(s) of the study, the subjects (people who participated in the study), the study's purpose, the results, and a discussion of its importance.

Look for the information in the reading you chose to complete the report form in your own words. Write only the key information in note form.

REPORT ON ANGER STUDIES

Topic of report: _____

Background

Purpose of research: _____

Author of study: _____

Conclusion: _____

Explanation of results: _____

_____

Other evidence: _____

_____

Discussion of Results

1. What has been learned: _____

2. Importance of the research: _____

_____

_____

Work with a partner who read the *same* article. Using your notes, take turns explaining the information in the important sections of the report.

After Reading

RETELLING THE INFORMATION: IS ANGER USEFUL OR DANGEROUS?

Work with a partner who took report notes from a *different* reading. Together, use your notes to explain the information. Based on the information from both readings, answer the following questions.

1. What two reactions to anger have a negative effect on health? Are these reactions similar or different?

   a. _____

   b. _____

2. What two health problems can people have as a result of their reactions to anger?

   a. _____

   b. _____

3. What is one technique that doctors recommend people use to cope with their negative reactions to anger?

   _____

4. Do researchers have evidence that these anger-related health problems can be solved or not?

   _____

REACTING: COMPARING STUDIES

Answer these questions based on the information from both studies and information of your own.

1. Is anger management important for people to know?
2. What are some techniques for anger management?
3. Can people learn to manage their anger?

DEBATING THE ISSUES

A. Consider this Situation: According to the readings so far, we know that anger is an emotion that is important to control and that controlling anger is not an easy task. With this in mind, consider the following question:

Should people be taught how to recognize and manage their emotions at a young age?

Discuss your ideas with others in a small group. Explain your ideas.

B. Propose or Oppose: Some schools are interested in teaching anger management to preschool-age children. Would you support this plan? To help make your decision, follow these steps.

1. Skim the following reading to find out some of the facts about this program.

THE NEW YORK TIMES

Primal Scream: Teaching Tykes to Get a Grip

By Doreen Carvajal

When educators gather this week in New Orleans for a national conference on teaching young children, Mother Goose rhymes will make room for lessons in anger management: aggression prevention, self-regulation and emotion control. . . .

Anger management programs for elementary school students have been around since the 1980s, but now teaching programs and lesson plans in "impulse control" are being offered to children so young they can't even lisp the words "temper tantrum."

Thus far, there is little data on the effectiveness of such coaching. Nevertheless, a debate is evolving about whether formal lessons should be delivered to all preschoolers or limited to children with problems controlling anger.

Even without conclusive evidence, some educators are willing to make a leap of logic: Why not offer lessons early since children experience the most rapid physical and mental growth between 3 and 6 years old? They also cite studies showing links between problem behavior in preschoolers and difficulties that continue through adolescence.

The programs, which rely on familiar nursery school tools like puppets, games,

books and flash cards, seek to provoke conversations about emotions. For example, some preschool teachers encourage children to express their feelings by drawing journals. Others organize childhood games with a twist (Simon says: I'm mad. Simon says: I'm happy.) One teacher asks children to dictate letters to their parents so she can tap their emotions; another discusses temper-tantrum management with readings of Maurice Sendak's classic *Where the Wild Things Are*.

"Good preschool teachers have always tried to help children understand their emotions and label things," said Donna Bryant, the leader of a preschool behavior research project at the University of North Carolina at Chapel Hill. "But we have a long way to go in helping people understand the best things they can do."

Some experts wonder if it doesn't make more sense to offer intensive training only to the children who need it the most. "This is a tough question," said Carroll E. Izard, a psychology professor at the University of Delaware, who has also been studying young children and whose findings have been used to create "emotion-centered prevention programs" in the Delaware towns of Symrna and Clayton. "Singling out the problem children for special treatment doesn't do much for their self-image. On the other hand, exposing the nonproblem children to the program will very probably cause them no difficulty."

. . .

Professor Izard and other researchers have measured the ability of children to recognize emotional expressions in other people. Based on that emotional skill, Professor Izard said they could actually predict negative and positive behaviors as the children reached the third grade. "A child that has more trouble recognizing cues is more likely to get into trouble," he said. "If you measure emotion knowledge and look at the social behavior later, we can predict social withdrawal and depression. Children who have trouble recognizing emotions are more likely to find themselves rejected or on the fringes."

Preschool teachers say that over the last 10 years they have noticed a shifting view of the need to address emotional skills, partly because many children come from families with more harried lives. But some preschool educators are wary of formal anger-management training because they believe teachers are already offering practical lessons in feelings.

2. Scan and highlight the information that explains the following points:
   a. What kinds of lessons are proposed?
   b. What age group will receive these lessons? Why are they appropriate for this age?
   c. What age group is already receiving instruction?
   d. Will the lessons be for all children or for a certain type of child?
   e. Why do teachers think it's important to teach emotional skills?

Work with a partner to explain the information you highlighted.

C. Debate: Decide whether you agree or disagree with teaching anger management to preschool-age children. Work with someone who shares your point of view.

Prepare to debate this question by following these steps:

1. Pair work: Make a list of the reasons you agree or disagree with the proposal.

2. Group work: Together, explain and add to your list of ideas. Think of examples to support each idea.

3. Pair work: Practice explaining your position.

4. Group work: Together, present and argue your position against others who disagree with you.

5. Group work: Make a list of all the reasons you agree and disagree with the proposal. Decide as a class what you think should be done.

Vocabulary Building

VOCABULARY IN CONTEXT

Use your understanding of one part of the sentence to help you guess the word that is missing. Complete each sentence with one of the phrases from the list.

a. adjusting for   b. come out   c. hold in
d. how to let off steam   e. make room for   f. play a role in

1. Psychologists believe that expressing our emotions can

   _____ reducing our pain.

2. Teachers think that it is important to help children learn

   _____ in ways that are not destructive.

3. Many people try to _____ their anger rather than let it out.

4. They changed the schedule in order to _____ some additional classes.

5. The scientists knew that news of their discovery would

   _____ eventually.

6. Researchers found important results even after

_____ the ages of the people in their study.

Check your answers. Work with a partner to read the sentences.

THE LANGUAGE OF EXAMPLES

In English, an important way to explain something is to give an example or two. Read these sentences. Write an *I* under the word that expresses the idea and an *E* under the word or phrase that contains the example.

1. Kawachi suggests stress-reduction strategies like meditation.

2. Anger releases stress hormones like adrenalin.

3. The programs rely on familiar nursery school tools like puppets, games, books and flash cards.

4. The school seeks to provoke conversations about emotions. For example, some preschool teachers encourage children to express their feeling by drawing journals.

5. Dwelling on anger increases its power; the body needs a chance to process the adrenaline through exercise, relaxation techniques, a well-timed intervention, or even the old admonition to "count to ten."

Check your answers with a partner. Take turns reading your sentences. Write three sentences of your own that show how an idea is explained through examples.

1. _____

2. _____

3. _____

◼ Expanding Your Language

SPEAKING

A. Interviewing: Answer the questionnaire on the topic of anger. Check your rating on page E–5 in the Exercise section. Interview two people who completed their questionnaires. Compare your information. Report on the similarities and differences to others in your class.

How Hostile Are You?

Find out how hostile you are on the road, in a supermarket line, and at the office by answering these questions, devised by Dr. Redford Williams of Duke University.

1. **I am in the express checkout line at the supermarket, where a sign reads: "No more than 10 items, please!"**

   A. I pick up a magazine to pass the time.

   B. I glance ahead to see if anyone has more than 10 items.

2. **My spouse, boyfriend or girlfriend is going to get me a birthday present.**

   A. I prefer to pick it out myself.

   B. I prefer to be surprised.

3. **Someone is speaking very slowly during a conversation.**

   A. I am apt to finish his or her sentences.

   B. I am apt to listen until he or she finishes.

4. **Someone treats me unfairly.**

   A. I usually forget it rather quickly.

   B. I am apt to keep thinking about it for hours.

5. **The person who cuts my hair trims off more than I wanted.**

   A. I tell him or her what a lousy job he or she did.

   B. I figure it'll grow back, and I resolve to give my instructions more forcefully next time.

6. **I am riding as a passenger in the front seat of a car.**

   A. I take the opportunity to enjoy the scenery.

   B. I try to stay alert for obstacles ahead.

7. **At times, I have to work with incompetent people.**

   A. I concentrate on my part of the job.

   B. Having to put up with them ticks me off.

8. **Someone bumps into me in a store.**

   A. I pass it off as an accident.

   B. I feel irritated at the person's clumsiness.

9. **Someone is hogging the conversation at a party.**

   A. I look for an opportunity to put him or her down.

   B. I soon move to another group.

10. **There is a really important job to be done.**

    A. I prefer to do it myself.

    B. I am apt to call on my friends or co-workers for help.

11. **Someone criticizes something I have done.**

    A. I feel annoyed.

    B. I try to decide whether the criticism is justified.

12. **Another driver butts ahead of me in traffic.**

    A. I usually flash my lights or honk my horn.

    B. I stay farther behind such driver.

13. **I see a very overweight person walking down the street.**

    A. I wonder why these people have such little self-control.

    B. I think that he or she might have a metabolic defect or a psychological problem.

14. **There have been times when I was very angry with someone.**

    A. I have always been able to stop short of hitting them.

    B. I have, on occasion, hit or shoved them.

15. **I recall something that angered me previously.**

    A. I feel angry all over again.

    B. The memory doesn't bother me nearly as much as the actual event did.

    –Laura Mansnerus,
    The New York Times Magazine

B. Discussion: Form a group with some classmates who are from different countries to exchange ideas based on the following questions.

1. What are some of the most common reasons that people get angry?
2. Is expressing anger the same in all cultures? If not, what are the differences?
3. Can anger be a positive force? Give some examples to support your opinion.

C. Reacting to Reading: Read the following story and find out about one woman's reaction of anger. As you read the story consider these questions; what made this woman angry? What was the result of her anger?

I'm Too Mad To Die!

By Bill DeFoore

A friend of mine named Dayna was on a backpacking trip in the Rockies when she learned the value of her own anger. She and her friend Lynn had been traveling around in an old Volkswagen bug for several weeks when they decided to hike up into the mountains and do some camping. Neither of them had much experience in this, but they were adventurous and carefree—a combination which almost proved deadly.

Lynn had seemed to be the one who had it all together during the trip. She was bold in talking to strangers, getting free meals and finding places to stay. Dayna was more shy and reserved, holding back in many situations where Lynn seemed brave and daring. Lynn's bravado led to some pretty hairy situations, but nothing compared to their experience on the mountain.

It was Lynn's idea to keep hiking, even when it started getting cold and the sun was settling behind the nearby snow-capped peaks. Dayna protested, but as usual, Lynn insisted. Soon it became apparent that they were in trouble.

They came to a place on the mountain where they could not go any higher. There were no more trees to hold onto and the slopes were getting steeper. Both of them were amateur climbers at best. They were not equipped to spend the night on the mountain, even if there had been a place to put a bedroll.

Suddenly Dayna noticed a change in Lynn. She got quiet and started making little whimpering sounds. Her hands and legs were starting to tremble. When she looked into Lynn's eyes, Dayna could actually see her collapsing inside.

Lynn whispered in a small, weak voice, "Dayna, I have to tell you something. I have a fear of heights."

"Now she tells me," thought Dayna.

Just at that moment, the mountain seemed to push against Lynn's backpack and dislodge her sleeping bag. Before Dayna could reach it, it was tumbling down the mountain.

Unsteady on their feet, they watched in silence as the sleeping bag bounced all the way into the ravine that stretched into the blackness below them. There was a moment of silence that seemed to vibrate with their fear. They were suddenly aware that their lives were hanging by a thread. Little did they know the thread that would save them was Dayna's anger.

A light snow started to fall and the wind picked up a little, making a low moaning sound. There was a desolate, lonely feeling in the air. Lynn seemed to be fading into the side of the cliff. But not Dayna.

Dayna felt herself getting hot inside. At first she didn't know what it was. Then she suddenly realized. She was furious! Without knowing what she was saying or why, Dayna started screaming at Lynn, at God and at the mountain. She told all three of them that her time was not up!

"I'm not ready to die!" she screamed, "And I sure don't plan to end my life on this cold, lonely mountain or tumbling down the side of it! I've come too far and been through too much to quit now!"

She stood up, grabbed Lynn's pack and slung it over her shoulder with her own. In a voice she barely recognized as hers, she said to Lynn, "Get up! We're going down!" Lynn was whining by now and not making much sense. She was terrified of the situation, but she was even more afraid of the rage in Dayna.

She was still talking about being afraid of heights when Dayna took her by the arm and pulled her up until they were face to face. Looking hard into Lynn's frightened eyes, Dayna said in a forceful and confident voice, "We are going down, because I'm taking us down. You are going to be just fine. Hold on to me and shut up."

Dayna had not felt so powerful since the time she beat up the neighborhood bully when she was eight years old. Anger had been her ally before and it came to her aid now. Her body felt strong and steady as she helped her trembling friend down the side of the mountain in the cold windy twilight. She did not really know what had happened and she didn't question it. Only years later did she realize that her anger had saved her life.

Although her life had been far from wonderful, Dayna was determined not to lose it. The result had been an empowering anger that allowed her to do exactly what needed to be done. Dayna discovered the survival value of her anger.

–Health Communications, Inc.

Work with a partner. Recount the details of this story to each other. Then discuss the questions you considered as you read. Finally, write two important questions of your own about this story for others to react to. Share your questions with the class.

WRITING

Journal Writing: Write your reactions to the ideas about anger that you read of in this chapter. What thoughts did you have about the information or in the discussions you had? Would you use any of this information in your life?

Topic Writing: Based on the information in this chapter and information of your own, write about the topic of anger, featuring three key points: (1) what researchers know about the emotion of anger, (2) how anger can harm, and (3) how useful anger can be.

CHAPTER 10

Getting through Life

Chapter Openers

AGREE/DISAGREE: ARE OPTIMISTS JUST BORN THAT WAY?

Circle *A* if you agree or *D* if you disagree

1. A   D   Most people are very happy most of the time.

2. A   D   Happy people are just born that way.

3. A   D   We can't change our basic personality.

4. A   D   People who are wealthy are happier than those with less money.

5. A   D   Most people expect to be happy in their lives.

6. A   D   People's feelings affect the amount of success in their lives.

Work with a partner or a small group. Compare your answers. Explain your answers as completely as possible.

Exploring and Understanding Reading

PREDICTING

Read all the following quotes taken from the reading. Brainstorm a list of ideas that each quote makes you think of. Some possibilities include guessing at the meaning, deciding whether you agree or disagree, or giving an example you know of. Write these ideas in note form.

Quote	*Ideas*
1. "Students with high hope set themselves higher goals and know how to work to attain them."	
2. "Having hope means you have both the will and the way to accomplish goals, whatever they may be."	
3. "It's not enough to wish for something, you need the means too."	
4. "Hope can be nurtured."	
5. "Where there's a will, there's a way."	

Discuss the ideas you brainstormed with a partner. Share your ideas with others.

Based on your work with these quotes, check (✔) the ideas you expect to find in this reading.

1. _____ The unimportance of having hope in order to be successful

2. _____ How successful people accomplish their goals

3. _____ Wanting good things to happen is enough

4. _____ The way to increase people's sense of hope

5. _____ Why hope is so important

Read the selection and then check your predictions. Discuss your answers with a partner.

THE NEW YORK TIMES

Hope Emerges as the Key to Success in Life

By Daniel Coleman

Psychologists are finding that hope plays a surprisingly potent role in giving people a measurable advantage in realms as diverse as academic achievement, bearing up in onerous jobs and coping with tragic illness. And, by contrast, the loss of hope is turning out to be a stronger sign that a person may commit suicide than other factors long thought to be more likely risks.

"Hope has proven a powerful predictor of outcome in every study we've done so far," said Dr. Charles R. Snyder, a psychologist at the University of Kansas who has devised a scale to assess how much hope a person has.

For example, in research with 3,920 college students, Dr. Snyder and his colleagues found that the level of hope among freshmen at the beginning of their first semester was a more accurate predictor of their college grades than were their S.A.T., scores or their grade point averages in high school, the two measures most commonly used to predict college performance. The study was reported in part in the November issue of *The Journal of Personality and Social Psychology.*

"Students with high hope set themselves higher goals and know how to work to attain them," Dr. Snyder said. "When you compare students of equivalent intellectual aptitude and past academic achievements, what sets them apart is hope."

In devising a way to assess hope scientifically, Dr. Snyder went beyond the simple notion that hope is merely the sense that everything will turn out all right. "That notion is not concrete enough, and it blurs two key components of hope," Dr.

Snyder said. "Having hope means believing you have both the will and the way to accomplish your goals, whatever they may be."

Getting Out of a Jam

The scale assesses people's sense of having the essential means by asking, for instance, whether they typically find they can think of many ways to get out of a jam or find ways to solve problems that discourage others. It measures will through such questions as whether people feel they have been fairly successful in life or usually pursue goals with great energy.

Despite the folk wisdom that "where there's a will there's a way," Dr. Snyder has found that the two are not necessarily connected. In a study of more than 7,000 men and women from 18 to 70 years old, Dr. Snyder discovered that only about 40 percent of people are hopeful in the technical sense of believing they typically have the energy and means to accomplish their goals, whatever those might be.

The study found that about 20 percent of the people believed in their ability to find the means to attain their goals, but said they had little will to do so. Another 20 percent have the opposite pattern, saying they had the energy to motivate themselves but little confidence that they would find the means.

The rest had little hope at all, reporting that they typically had neither the will nor the way.

"It's not enough just to have the wish for something," said Dr. Snyder. "You need the means, too. On the other hand, all the skills to solve a problem won't help if you don't have the willpower to do it."

Dr. Snyder found that people with high levels of hope share several attributes:

- Unlike people who are low in hope, they turn to friends for advice on how to achieve their goals.

- They tell themselves they can succeed at what they need to do.

- Even in a tight spot, they tell themselves things will get better as time goes on.

- They are flexible enough to find different ways to get to their goals.

- If hope for one goal fades, they aim for another. "Those low in hope tend to become fixated on one goal and persist even when they find themselves blocked," Dr. Snyder said. "They just stay at it and get frustrated."

- They show an ability to break a formidable task into specific, achievable chunks. "People low in hope see only the large goal, and not the small steps to it along the way," Dr. Snyder said.

In a 10-year study of 206 patients who reported thoughts of suicide but had not yet made an attempt, the patients' scores on the hopelessness scale was the single best predictor of whether they would go on to attempt suicide, Dr. Beck reported in a 1987 article in *The American Journal of Psychiatry*.

People who get a high score on the hope scale "have had as many hard times as those with low scores, but have learned to think about it in a hopeful way, seeing a setback as a challenge, not a failure," Dr. Snyder said.

He and his colleagues are trying to design programs to help children develop the ways of thinking found in hopeful people. "They've often learned their mental habit of hopefulness from a specific person, like a friend or teacher," Dr. Snyder said.

"Hope can be nurtured," he said. Dr. Snyder has made a videotape for that purpose, showing interviews with students who are high on hope, to help freshmen better handle the stress of their first year.

In a study by Dr. Lori Irving, a psychologist at the Palo Alto Veterans Affairs Hospital in California, women who viewed a videotape about cancer that had a hopeful script did more to change their health habits in a positive way, like getting Pap smears and quitting smoking, than did women who saw another one with the same information but without the positive wording.

The effect of the hopeful videotape was strongest on the women who had gotten a low score on the hopefulness scale. Dr. Snyder said similar approaches might work to raise hopefulness among children in impoverished neighborhoods.

Understanding the Details

A. INFERENCE

READING TIP: An inference is an idea that you might logically think could be true, based on the information in a reading, even though it is not directly stated. Considering what can be inferred from a reading is an important critical reading skill.

Read each of the following statements. Write *T* if an idea is stated in the reading, *F* if it is not stated or is untrue, and *I* if you think the statement can be inferred. Mark the question number in the margin where you located the information in the reading.

1. _____ Having hope is important for success in a variety of life situations.

2. _____ Dr. Charles Snyder's scale for assessing hope would be a useful tool for university admissions offices to use.

3. _____ Dr. Snyder would like to test many more students at different universities.

4. _____ According to Dr. Snyder, you have to have both the will and the way to accomplish your goals.

5. _____ Hopeful people are friendlier than those without hope.

6. _____ Hopeful people are good at giving themselves positive messages.

7. _____ Hopeful people never give up trying to accomplish a goal even when it seems hopeless.

8. _____ Hopeful people see only the large goal.

9. _____ Dr. Snyder's scale can be used to by crisis centers to determine if a person is a suicide risk.

10. _____ Dr. Snyder believes that hopefulness can be taught to children.

Work with a partner to compare your answers. Refer to the reading to check where you found the information on which you based your answer.

B. CHARTING RESULTS

Making a chart is a useful way to critically analyze the information in this type of reading. Use the chart headings to help you locate the key information. Report on the results of the studies only. Write the information in note form.

Results of Studies that Show the Importance of Hope		
Study	Author	Results
Research with 3,920 college students		
Research of more than 7,000 men and women		40% 20% 20% rest 6 attributes of hopeful people

Study	Author	Results
10-year study of 206 patients		
Women viewing cancer video		

Work with a partner to take turns explaining the results of the studies.

After Reading

APPLYING THE INFORMATION: SOLVING A PROBLEM

According to the information in "Hope Emerges as the Key to Success in Life," the most effective messages give specific information on the way to accomplish goals and do so in a positive way.

A. Look at the following situations and circle the messages you think are the most effective.

1. Your friend, Sue Kwan, is in her freshman year at university. She is disappointed because she got a "C" grade on her first paper. Sue tells you that she is thinking of dropping the course. She thinks she's a bad student and that her writing is awful. You tell Sue the following:

   a. It's better to drop the course before the deadline.

   b. Don't worry, you'll do better on the next paper.

   c. Ask your professor why you got a "C" and find out what you can do to improve.

2. Your friend, Roberto Sanchez, has started to study art. Roberto really likes it but his parents are afraid that it will take time from his math and science courses. He is worried that his parents will be disappointed in him if he continues. Roberto thinks that he could be a really good artist if he continues, but he also thinks that his parents may be right. You tell Roberto the following:

a. Pleasing your parents is more important than doing something that pleases you.

b. Studying art might not lead to a good job in the future. It's better to concentrate on math and science.

c. Look at your weekly schedule and see how much free time you have. Decide if you could have time to do both art and your other studies. Then decide on a week-by-week basis.

3. Your friend, Judy Lee, has been feeling anxious and has trouble sleeping at night. She thinks she has heart problems but is afraid to see a doctor. You tell Judy the following:

a. Don't worry. It's all in your mind. Have a glass of wine at dinner and relax.

b. I would be worried if I were you. Your life is too stressful

c. I'll help you to find a good doctor and schedule an appointment. If I'm free, I'll go with you to the doctor's office.

B. Discuss your choices with a partner or in a small group. Based on what you remember from the reading, give reasons for your answers.

APPLYING THE INFORMATION: ACHIEVING OUR GOALS

In the reading "Hope Emerges as the Key to Success in Life" we learned that people achieve their goals when they have the will and the opportunity to do so, and include the following:

1. Encouragement of friends and family
2. Practical experience of carrying out a task
3. Ability to set high goals and a willingness to work for them
4. Development of positive mental habits

A. The next reading gives some statements about these ideas. Read the article, and then reread it critically to see if any of the four ideas are found in the information.

Look for any information that fits in the four categories. Mark the number in the margin next to the information.

LONDON DAILY TELEGRAPH

Practice, not talent, produces "genius"

By John Clare

LONDON—The notion that geniuses such as Shakespeare, Mozart and Picasso were "gifted" or possessed innate talents is a myth, according to a study by a British psychologist.

After examining outstanding performances in the arts and sport, Professor Michael Howe and colleagues at Exeter University concluded that excellence is determined by opportunities, encouragement, training, motivation, self-confidence and—most of all—practice.

The theory—a radical break with traditional beliefs—has been applauded by academics worldwide.

It has significant implications for teachers and parents, not least because children who are not thought to be gifted are being denied the encouragement they need to succeed.

The authors took as their starting point the "widespread belief that to reach high levels of ability a person must possess an innate potential called talent." They said it was important to establish whether the belief was correct because it had social and educational consequences affecting selection procedures and training.

However, studies of accomplished artists and mathematicians, top tennis players and swimmers reported few early signs of promise prior to parental encouragement.

No case was found of anyone reaching the highest levels of achievement without devoting thousands of hours to serious training.

Even those who were believed to be exceptionally talented, whether in music, mathematics, chess or sports, required lengthy periods of instruction and practice.

Mozart Received Training

Mozart produced his best work only after a long period of training. It was not until he had been immersed in music for 16 years that he first produced an acknowledged masterwork.

"The early biographies of prominent composers have revealed that they all received intensive and regular supervised practice sessions over a period of several years," the study said. "The emergence of unusual skills typically followed rather than preceded a period during which unusual opportunities were provided, often combined with strong expectations that a child would do well."

"The persistent myth that some people reach high levels of performance without devoting numerous hours to practice owes much to the fact that practicing activities are usually outside the casual observer's view."

Research had shown strong correlations between the level of performance of student violinists and the number of hours they practiced. Even people who were not thought to have special talent could, after training, reach levels previously considered attainable only by gifted individuals.

Research had shown that cocktail waitresses could regularly remember as many as 20 drink orders at a time, far more than a control group of university students. "It is conceivable that people who are employed as waiters gravitate to such jobs because of an inborn memory skill," the study said. "But the findings make it far more likely that employees excel in recording orders because of on-the-job practice."

In sport, differences in the composition of certain muscles were thought to be reliable predictors of differences in athletic performance.

"However, the differences in the proportion of slow-twitch muscle fibres that are essential for success in long-distance running are largely the result of extended practice in running."

The study said reasoning about talent was often circular. "She plays so well because she has a talent. How do I know she has a talent? That's obvious, she plays so well."

Some children did acquire ability more effortlessly than others but that did not mean they were gifted.

Rare Performance Standards

Categorizing children as innately talented is discriminatory, the authors say, "preventing people from pursuing a goal because of the unjustified conviction of teachers or parents that certain children would not benefit from the opportunities given to those who are deemed to be talented."

By the same token, a false belief that one did not possess the necessary talent could affect a person negatively. Talent was a myth and it was time it was demolished,

say the authors, but they add that it would be wrong to assume that any diligent child could excel at anything, especially in the absence of expert teaching, encouragement, and unusual motivation.

Opponents of Howe's theory said practice and other factors were no doubt important contributors to outstanding performance, but not enough to explain great creative works.

"Talent is essential," said David Feldman and Tamar Katzir of Tufts University, Massachusetts.

B. Work with a partner. Compare the information you marked for each of the categories. Refer to the reading in cases where you disagree.

Discuss the following question.

What positive points are explained in this article
    for children?
    for parents?
    for teachers?
    for athletes?
    for musicians?

▨ Building Vocabulary

VOCABULARY IN CONTEXT

Words you already know can help you understand the meaning of new words. Write the meanings of the words *in boldface* in your own words. Circle the words that helped you guess the meaning.

1. Psychologists are finding that hope plays a role in **realms as diverse** as academic achievement, bearing up in onerous jobs, and coping with tragic illness.

   Meaning: _____

2. "Hope has proven a powerful predictor of outcome in every study we've done so far," said Dr. Charles R. Snyder . . . who has **devised a scale to assess** how much hope a person has.

   Meaning: _____

3. "When you compare students of **equivalent intellectual aptitude** and past academic achievements, what sets them apart is hope."

   Meaning: _____

4. "Those low in hope tend to **become fixated** on one goal and persist even when they find themselves blocked."

   Meaning: _____

5. They show an ability to break a **formidable** task into specific, achievable chunks.

   Meaning: _____

6. "Hope can be **nurtured**," said Dr. Snyder, who has made a videotape showing interviews with students who are high on hope, to help freshmen better handle the stress of their first year.

   Meaning: _____

WORD FORMS: ADVERBS

Adverbs are parts of speech that tell us about the how of things. Adverbs modify verbs, adjectives, or other adverbs. Many adverbs end in *-ly*.

A. Read each statement. Circle the adverb. Write *V* if the adverb modifies a verb, *ADJ* if it modifies an adjective, or *ADV* if it modifies an adverb.

1. _____ Psychologists are finding that hope plays a surprisingly potent role in giving people a measurable advantage.

2. _____ In devising a way to assess hope scientifically, Dr. Snyder went beyond a simple notion.

3. _____ The scale assesses people . . . by asking whether they typically find they can think of many ways to get out of a jam.

4. _____ It measures will through such questions as whether people feel they have been fairly successful in life or usually pursue goals with great energy.

5. _____ Dr. Snyder has found that the two are not necessarily connected.

Expanding Your Language

SPEAKING

Simulation: Role Play

To prepare this simulation, choose to work with others and prepare one of the following situations. Choose Scenario A, which follows, or Scenario B on Exercise page E–6 at the end of the book.

Scenario A

Consider the following situation. Read the information and decide what action you would recommend and why. Compare your solution to that of others. Together, write out lines of dialogue to role play the situation and your solution.

You work at a bookstore. You work with someone who always seems to be in a bad mood. The person is sometimes rude when you ask a question, even though he has worked there much longer and knows the store better than you do. This coworker never wants to help you or to let you help. Even though you try to be pleasant and begin conversations, your efforts are ignored. This person has even insulted you in front of the other workers in the store. One day you find out that this person is being considered for a new and better job as a manager at the store. The company wants you to give your evaluation of this person as part of the decision-making process. You will be meeting with the head of personnel to give your recommendation. What would your evaluation be?

Step 1: Work with your partners and discuss your recommendation.

Step 2: Prepare the lines of dialogue between the following people:
  a. Pleasant bookstore worker
  b. Unpleasant bookstore worker
  c. Other employees
  d. Personnel director

Step 3: Use your lines to act out the story, but do not memorize the lines. Be creative.

Step 4: Following your role play, ask the class to complete the following evaluation sheet for the personnel director, who will recommend the bookstore worker for a promotion or not.

The candidate would be:
_____ A. Outstanding in this position
_____ B. Good in this position
_____ C. Suitable in this position
_____ D. Unsuited for this position

WRITING

A. Journal Entry: Write in your journal about the topic of attitude. How do you feel your attitude has helped you or will help you to achieve your goals? Think about a person in your life who has inspired or encouraged you to be the best you could be. Think about the opportunities you believe exist for people to develop and maintain a positive attitude. Look for newspaper articles on this topic over the next few weeks and write your reaction to them.

B. Topic Writing: Write about the importance of attitude in our lives based on your discussions and chapter readings. Follow these steps:

1. Outline the ideas about (a) the importance of hope, (b) what hope is, (c) the areas of life that are affected by our attitude, and (d) how to nurture hope. Include at least three or four points under each of these ideas.
2. Write about each idea in a separate paragraph.

Read On: Taking It Further

A DIFFERENT POINT OF VIEW

You may know someone who is almost always upbeat and positive. It may be hard to understand how someone can be so happy—and if you know this person well, it may even be a bit annoying. The next reading is a very personal story of how one person learned about the importance of attitude.

A. Read the story and prepare to discuss the following questions.

1. What was Jerry's answer to the question "How do you do it?" What is your reaction to this advice?
2. What are the feelings you experienced as you read this story?
3. What does this story tell us about the nature of life?

Attitude Is Everything

by Francie Baltazar-Schwartz

Jerry was the kind of guy you love to hate. He was always in a good mood and always had something positive to say. When someone would ask him how he was doing, he would reply, "If I were any better, I would be twins!"

He was a unique manager because he had several waiters who had followed him around from restaurant to restaurant. The reason the waiters followed Jerry was because of his attitude. He was a natural motivator. If an employee was having a bad day, Jerry was there telling the employee how to look on the positive side of the situation. Seeing this style really made me curious, so one day I went up to Jerry and asked him, "I don't get it! You can't be a positive person all of the time. How do you do it?"

Jerry replied, "Each morning I wake up and say to myself, 'Jerry, you have two choices today. You can choose to be in a good mood or you can choose to be in a bad mood.' I choose to be in a good mood. Each time something bad happens, I can choose to be a victim or I can choose to learn from it. I choose to learn from it. Every time someone comes to me complaining, I can choose to accept their complaining or I can point out the positive side of life. I choose the positive side of life."

"Yeah, right, it's not that easy," I protested.

"Yes it is," Jerry said. "Life is all about choices. When you cut away all the junk, every situation is a choice. You choose how you react to situations. You choose how people will affect your mood. You choose to be in a good mood or a bad mood. The bottom line: It's your choice how you live life." I reflected on what Jerry said. Soon thereafter, I left the restaurant industry to start my own business. We lost touch, but I often thought about him when I made a choice about life instead of reacting to it.

Several years later, I heard that Jerry did something you are never supposed to do in a restaurant business: he left the back door open one morning and was held up at gunpoint by three armed robbers. While trying to open the safe, his hand, shaking from nervousness, slipped off the combination. The robbers panicked and shot him. Luckily, Jerry was found relatively quickly and rushed to the local trauma center. After 18 hours of surgery and weeks of intensive care, Jerry was released from the hospital with fragments of the bullets still in his body. I saw Jerry about six months after the accident. When I asked him how he was, he replied, "If I were any better, I'd be twins. Wanna see my scars?"

I declined to see his wounds, but did ask him what had gone through his mind as the robbery took place. "The first thing that went through my mind was that I should have locked the back door," Jerry replied. "Then, as I lay on the floor, I remembered that I had two choices: I could choose to live, or I could choose to die. I chose to live."

"Weren't you scared? Did you lose consciousness?" I asked.

Jerry continued, "The paramedics were great. They kept telling me I was going to be fine. But when they wheeled me into the emergency room and I saw the expressions on the faces of the doctors and nurses, I got really scared. In their eyes, I read, 'He's a dead man,' I knew I needed to take action."

"What did you do?" I asked.

"Well, there was a big, burly nurse shouting questions at me," said Jerry. "She asked if I was allergic to anything. 'Yes,' I replied. The doctors and nurses stopped working as they waited for my reply. I took a deep breath and yelled, 'Bullets!' Over their laughter, I told them, 'I am choosing to live. Operate on me as if I am alive, not dead.'"

Jerry lived thanks to the skills of his doctors, but also because of his amazing attitude. I learned from him that every day we have the choice to live fully. Attitude, after all, is everything.

B. Write your reactions to this story in your reading journal.

■ *READING TIP: Don't forget to write your reading journal and vocabulary log entries in your notebook.*

Health
Matters

Health is a blessing that money cannot buy

– Izaak Walton

215

Introducing the Topics

Scientists and physicians have made a lot of progress in diagnosing and dealing with many of the problems from which the human body can suffer. At the same time, however, many social and ethical issues are raised. This unit deals with two areas in particular. Chapter 11 looks at organ transplants, and Chapter 12 focuses on having babies.

Points of Interest

PROVERBS

The following proverbs are from different parts of the world. Read and add any more that you can think of. Discuss what each one means with a partner or in a small group.

1. *Sickness comes on horseback and departs on foot.* (Dutch)

2. *Sleep to the sick is half death.* (German)

3. *Show him death and he will be content with fever.* (Persian)

4. *However broken down is the spirit's shrine, the spirit is there all the same.* (Nigerian)

5. _____

6. _____

DISCUSSION

1. What do you know about the symptoms and treatments of each of the following problems?

   ■ Heart disease   ■ Leukemia   ■ Diabetes
   ■ AIDS   ■ Inability to have children

2. Do you know anybody who suffers from one of these problems?
3. Has your experience with medical doctors in general been positive or negative? Give examples to support your answer.

CHAPTER **11**

Transplants

Chapter Openers

DISCUSSION QUESTIONS

Think about the following questions. Share your ideas with a partner or in a small group.

1. What is a transplant?
2. Which parts of the body can be transplanted?
3. What are some problems associated with transplants?
4. Have you or has anyone that you know had a transplant? If you answer yes, describe what happened.

What is Your Opinion? Agree or Disagree
A. The demand for organs has always been higher than the supply. As a result, certain choices have to be made. The following statements deal with some of these choices. Circle *A* if you agree or *D* if you disagree with the statement.

1. A D Young people should be chosen before old people.

2. A D A patient who has had an unsuccessful transplant should be placed at the bottom of the list.

3. A D People whose disease has been caused by their life styles, (for example, alcoholics, smokers, addicts) should be given the same chance as everybody else.

4. A   D   People who suffer from a mental disability should not be allowed a transplant because they will not be able to follow the required steps after the operation.

B. Because the supply is so low, certain solutions have been suggested. Which of the following do you agree/disagree with?

1. A   D   People should be able to sell their organs.

2. A   D   Organs of a dead person should be automatically used unless that person has stated otherwise.

3. A   D   The brain is the most important organ in the body, so once people are brain dead they should be considered dead and their organs used instead of keeping these individuals indefinitely on life support.

Work with a partner or in a small group. Compare your ideas. Be ready to support your position with reasons and explanations if possible.

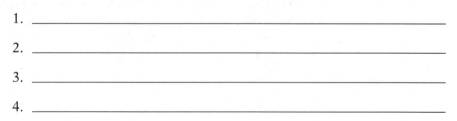

Exploring and Understanding Reading

PREVIEWING

The following article is taken from a weekly newsmagazine that gives information about people and ideas. Look at the title and subtitle of the article and make a list of four ideas you expect to find in the reading.

1. _____

2. _____

3. _____

4. _____

Share your ideas with a partner.

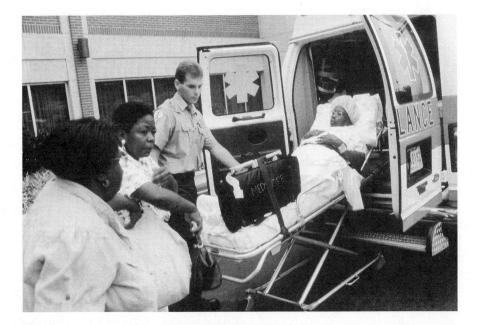

His Daughter's Gift of Life

By Bill Hewitt

A few years ago, Chet Szuber received the heart of his youngest child, Patti, who had been killed in a car accident; now, with each passing day, he celebrates her spirit.

1. Friendly but taciturn, Chet Szuber is not one to show much emotion. Yet even now, long after an event that changed virtually everything for him and his family, he cannot help choking up when discussing it. At a gathering for surviving members of the families of organ donors, Szuber, a 63-year-old Christmas tree farmer, gets up to thank the next of kin of those who died, on behalf of all organ recipients. "Without you," he says with emotion, "there wouldn't be any people like me." It is an equation Szuber understands only too well. For as he stands there with tears in his eyes, his daughter Patti's heart beats in his chest.

2. It has been five years since Chet Szuber made the most tragic sort of history, becoming the first person ever to receive the heart of his own child. Having suffered for years with chronic cardiac problems, he got the transplant on August 22, 1994, four days after Patti, then 22 and an aspiring nurse, died from injuries sustained in a car crash while she was vacationing in Tennessee's Smoky Mountains. Since then he has tried to honor her memory as best he can by becoming an evangelist for organ donation. "Medical people tell me that they can speak all they want about donation," says Szuber, "but until you have somebody who has experienced it, it doesn't have the impact."

3. Patti was only a year old in 1972, when Szuber, then 36 and a salesman at Sears, had his first heart attack and was out of work for nine months. In the years that followed, he had two more attacks and had to quit his job. By the time she was 20, Patti was often her father's chauffeur, driving him from their home in the Detroit suburb of Berkley up to the tree farm he had started on family land in northern Michigan. In 1990, Szuber was put on the waiting list for a heart transplant, which seemed to offer his last hope for survival. But as years went by and no heart came his way, he got to a point where he could barely move around during the day. "I had kind of given up," he says, "I had waited so long." Her father's problems profoundly affected Patti, who decided to go into the medical field, her family believes, because of all she had seen him go through. In 1994 she set her sights on getting a degree as a surgical assistant.

4. She was scheduled to start classes within days when she went on her last vacation with childhood friend Todd Herbst, then 24. Early on August 18, their car skidded off a curving road in the Smokies, and Patti, not wearing a seat belt, was thrown from the vehicle. By the time the Szubers—Chet, his wife Jeanne, now 63, and their five other children—got to the University of Tennessee Medical Center at Knoxville, to which Patti had been airlifted, she was on life support with no hope of recovery. Her family remembered that she had once casually mentioned that she had filled out an organ-donor card, so they gave the hospital the go-ahead to do whatever was necessary to get her organs to needy recipients. On August 21, Patti was declared brain dead. Susan Fredenberg Cross, a donor coordinator who had learned of Szuber's condition, gently suggested that he could get his daughter's heart, since donor families are allowed to direct organs to eligible friends and kin. Szuber refused. "I didn't think it was right," he says. "And I wasn't sure I could stand every heartbeat reminding me of Patti." Finally, though, Jeanne and his other children prevailed on him to accept. Patti's kidneys and liver were given to other recipients, and within 24 hours her heart was beating in Szuber.

5. He missed his daughter's funeral back in Berkley, because he was in the hospital recovering from the operation. After that there was a long period of physical rehabilitation and a longer time getting used to the idea of what had happened to him. "He was fine physically, but he was emotionally upset," says his son Bob, 41. "He felt he was going to be looked upon as a freak." Szuber, who is now able to hunt, fish and play golf, decided that a way to deal with his lingering grief was to become an advocate, raising awareness of the need for organ donors. Every year he gives a dozen speeches around the country, imploring people to sign up and lobbying for changes in donation procedures. Yet he remains haunted by Patti's tragedy. Unlike most other transplant recipients, Szuber has never celebrated the customary "second birthday"—the day on which recipients begin their lives anew with donated organs. "It's hard to celebrate a life and death at the same time," says Jeanne, "so we just kind of forgot about it."

6. But those who benefited from the generosity of Patti and her family cannot forget. Thanks to Patti's kidney, Mary Lawery, 57, a retired nanny in Nashville, now lives a relatively normal life, free of dialysis. Lawery, who has met the Szubers twice, knows she can never repay her debt to them. "It makes you sad because they loved her so much," she says. Meanwhile, Shirley Cobb Dotson, 21, from Memphis, perhaps gained the most from Patti. She had suffered from liver trouble from the age of 13, and in August 1994 she had been given only 72 hours to live, when Patti's donor liver arrived—"I pray every morning and night," says Dotson, "and I keep thanking God for this miracle." It is a feeling Chet Szuber knows well but always with that heartbreaking twist. "It's such a bittersweet situation. I certainly appreciate the good health," he says, "but I sure do miss that kid."

–People

SURVEYING

Read the first two paragraphs (introduction) and the first sentence of every paragraph after that. Underline the key words in each sentence. Using these key words, write the main idea of each paragraph in the margin. Try to use as few words as possible for each idea. Using your previewing and your surveying fill in the following table.

Paragraph	Main Idea
1, 2	*Introduction*
3	
4	
5	
6	

Share your ideas with a partner or in a small group.

SCANNING FOR DETAILS

Read the following questions. Use the list of main ideas to help you decide which paragraph the answer is in. Underline the answer and then write it in your own words and in note form.

1. What is so unique about Chet Szuber?

   _____

2. How old was Patti when her father had his first heart attack?

   _____

3. What major decision did Patti make as a result of her father's condition?

   _____

4. What made Patti's family decide to donate her organs?

   _____

5. How did Szuber react to receiving his daughter's heart?

   _____

6. Give as many examples as you can to show that Szuber is physically in good condition.

_____

7. Who gained the most from Patti and why?

_____

Compare your answers with a partner or in a small group. Refer to the information you underlined in the reading if necessary.

REACTING TO THE INFORMATION

Discuss the following with a partner.

1. Imagine that there had been another patient in the same area, but in a much more serious condition than Patti's father. Who should have priority?
2. One person died and that person's organ donation allowed three others to live normal lives.
   a. How does this affect the way we look at organ donation?
   b. How does this affect the way that organ recipients lead the rest of their lives?

PAIRED READINGS

■ **READING TIP:**
Remember!
Newspaper articles have very short paragraphs and therefore surveying to get the main ideas is not very useful. The best strategy is to skim.

The following are newspaper articles dealing with different ethical issues that have been raised about organ transplants. Choose one of the readings. Work with a partner who is reading the *same* article.

■■

Reading 1: Live and Let Die Over Transplants

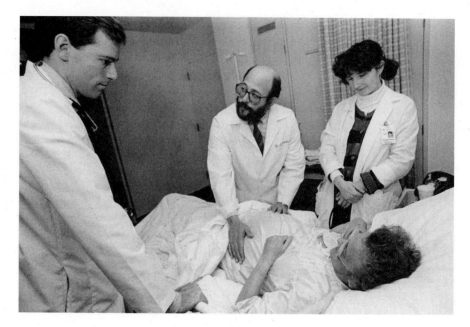

SKIMMING

Read the article quickly and answer the following questions.

1. Which aspect of transplants does this article focus on?

   ■ Supply: the consequences of there not being enough organs available

   ■ Demand: the consequences of having too many people waiting for organs

2. What are three reasons why some people who need organs do not even get put on the waiting list?

   a. _____

   b. _____

   c. _____

Compare your information with your partner. Refer to the reading to support your answer.

THE NEW YORK TIMES

Live and Let Die Over Transplants

By Cheryl Gay Stolberg

1. The day Dr. Philip Bach met Sandra Jensen, more than 10 years ago, he knew that she would someday need a new heart and lung. Ms. Jensen had Down syndrome, which left her with a defective heart that was ruining her lungs. "I figured we'd carry her as long as possible," said Dr. Bach, a cardiologist in Sacramento, California, "and when the time came, we'd get her a heart-lung transplant."

2. The time came in 1995, when Ms. Jensen was 34. But when Dr. Bach tried to sign her up for a transplant, the medical centers at Stanford University and the University of California at San Diego rejected her sight unseen. The reason: low IQ. Doctors wouldn't risk wasting scarce organs on someone who might not be able to follow the complicated regimen of post-transplant drugs.

3. They picked the wrong woman to reject. Ms. Jensen was a lifelong advocate for the mentally disabled. She and her friends raised a ruckus. Both medical centers eventually relented, and she got her transplant at Stanford in 1996, although she died 16 months later of complications unrelated to her mental disability.

4. Ms. Jensen's experience offers a look into the live-or-die decision making that determines who gets a donated organ. Most of the controversy that we hear about has to do with how to determine who on the waiting list should get the next available organ. Ms. Jensen, however, is an example of the tens of thousands who never even get on that list.

Eliminating

6. According to a recent survey, roughly half of the 138,000 people who needed hearts, lungs, livers, kidneys and pancreases were listed for transplant, and fewer than one quarter of those received organs. According to Dr. Roger Evans, a health policy analyst at the Mayo Clinic, transplant centers don't like to say why they exclude patients but the reasons are many.

7. There is what Dr. Clive Callender, director of the transplant center at Howard University here, calls "the green screen." A new liver can cost as much as $250,000, and most hospitals want evidence of insurance up front. Racial minorities, who are less likely than whites to have medical coverage, are thus less likely to receive a referral for transplant surgery, Dr. Callender said.

8. Nor does insurance guarantee a referral. Doctors are also reluctant to transplant organs into someone with a complicated illness, fearing the patient will not survive. Ruth Dmitrzak of Pittsburgh learned she had liver disease in 1990, but her doctors never suggested a transplant, her son Gary said. When his mother's health started failing, he insisted that she be evaluated for a new liver. The University of Pittsburgh accepted Mrs. Dmitrzak as a candidate but later took her off the list when she grew sicker. She died a few months later, at 67 years old.

9. Most transplant centers also require "family support"—a network of people who can help patients through the complicated and tedious recovery.

Ethical Dilemmas

10. Those who do get referred undergo physical and psychological evaluation. The government, in its new regulation, is demanding uniform criteria for determining transplant prospects. Standards now vary from hospital to hospital.

11. For the surgeons, nurses, psychiatrists, and social workers performing these evaluations, the ethical dilemmas are endless. Should alcoholics, whose livers have been destroyed after years of hard drinking, be put on the list, for new livers? Most transplant surgeons say yes—if the patient has not had a drink for at least six months.

12. What about people who try to kill themselves by overdosing on Tylenol, which causes acute liver failure? "We try to avoid it like the plague," said Dr. Charles Miller, director of transplantation, at Mount Sinai Medical Center in New York City. "But if it's a teenager, what do you do?"

13. There is heated debate about whether prisoners deserve a spot on the list. Some transplant programs exclude them because they might not participate in follow-up care—an argument that Dr. James S. Levenson, a professor of psychiatry, medicine, and surgery at the Medical College of Virginia, says is invalid, since prisoners are relatively easy to find.

14. Age discrimination is another issue. At Mt. Sinai, Dr. Miller said, the standard is physiological age; in other words even a 75-year-old can get a new liver as long as he/she is otherwise healthy. At Stanford University, the age cutoff for lungs is 60. "If we had all the organs in the world, we would transplant everybody," said Dr. James Theodore, medical director of the medical center's heart and lung transplant center.

15. Dr. Theodore supervised the team that first rejected, then accepted, Ms. Jensen. In the wake of her transplant, Stanford no longer turns away mentally disabled people without first examining them. "We rejected her out of hand, based on a label," Dr. Theodore said. "That was wrong, and I'm willing to admit that."

SCANNING FOR IMPORTANT INFORMATION: UNDERLINING

Underline the answers to the following questions.

Ms. Jensen

1. What is Ms. Jensen's background?
2. What happened when she applied for a transplant?
3. What was her reaction?
4. What was the result?
5. What is Ms. Jensen an example of?

Eliminating

1. What percentage of those who need a transplant are on the waiting list?
2. How much can a liver transplant cost?
3. What are the consequences of this?
4. Why was Mrs. Dmitzrak taken off the list?
5. What other reason is mentioned for not accepting people on the list?

Ethical Dilemmas

1. What is the position on alcoholics? On attempted suicides
2. What is the argument against including prisoners?
3. How are Mt. Sinai and Stanford different in terms of age criteria?

Conclusion

How does Dr. Theodore feel about his original decision with respect to Ms. Jensen?

Compare what you underlined with your partner. Try to agree on what you think is important information. Make any changes that are necessary.

RECAPPING THE INFORMATION: NOTE TAKING

Fill in the following outline using only the information you underlined. Use your own words as much as possible.

Main Ideas	Details
A. Ms. Jensen background	_____
	_____
request for transplant	_____
response	_____
	_____
reaction	_____
result	_____
	_____
B. Eliminating survey	_____
	_____
Reasons for eliminating patients money	_____
	_____
too sick	_____
	_____
family support	_____
	_____

C. Ethical Dilemmas
alcoholics   _____

_____

attempted suicides   _____

_____

prisoners   _____

_____

age   _____

_____

D. Conclusion   _____

_____

Use your notes to talk about the article to each other. Make sure you use complete sentences and explain as much as possible.

REACTING TO THE INFORMATION

Find these quotes in the article and discuss them with your partner. Refer to the context in which they appear

1. "We try to avoid it . . . . But if it's a teenager, what do you do?"
2. "If we had all the organs in the world, we would transplant everybody."
3. "We rejected her out of hand, based on a label. That was wrong, and I'm willing to admit that."

■■
_____

Reading 2: Transplants Spark Grisly Debate

SKIMMING

Read the article quickly and answer the following questions.

1. Which aspect of transplants does this article focus on?

    - Supply: the consequences of there not being enough organs available
    - Demand: the consequences of having too many people waiting for organs

2. What three groups of people are involved in this debate on brain death?

    a. _____

    b. _____

    c. _____

Compare your information with your partner. Refer to the reading to support your answer.

Transplants Spark Grisly Debate

By Mark Kennedy

1. A health committee was holding public hearings to examine ways to improve Canada's low rate of organ donation. So far the committee had mostly heard from medical experts and patients who told sad stories about how people died while awaiting organ transplants.

2. At one point, however, officials were confronted with a different dilemma: from an ethical standpoint, are too many organs already being transplanted?

3. The committee was told that doctors are removing organs for transplant from "brain-dead" patients who are actually still alive.

4. The controversial testimony came from a small group of doctors—including one who once had a clinical near-death experience herself—and this started a fierce debate on the ethics of transplant medicine.

5. Critics of transplants complained the medical profession has made a fundamental moral mistake in allowing organs to be removed from patients who are still breathing but whose brains are declared to be clinically dead.

6. "I'm living testimony that people survive," said Ruth Oliver, a psychiatrist who suffered internal bleeding of the brain after childbirth in 1977. For a time, she said, she was deemed clinically dead by the doctors at the hospital but emerged from her condition and was regarded as a "miracle patient."

7. She told officials her experience demonstrates that practitioners of transplant medicine should proceed with caution.

"The value of each human soul created goes beyond what doctors can or cannot test of the functioning of the brain," she said.

"Unconscious or dying people are not people of lesser value. More and more ethicists, philosophers and churches are rejecting brain death specifically for that reason."

8. Until 1968, physicians waited until a donor actually stopped breathing or their heart stopped before they would remove a donor's organ. But since then, it has become ethically acceptable for physicians to perform such surgery if the lungs and heart are still functioning but the brain is clinically dead. In these instances, the brain is demonstrating no electrical activity and blood flow.

9. Michael Brear, a general practitioner, told officials the criteria used to diagnose brain death are seriously flawed.

"The so-called 'beating-heart cadavers' who are used as donors are, in fact, living patients. They are sick, they are dying. They are living and not dead."

But others disagreed.

No Moral Problems

10. Rabbi Reuven Bulka, chairman of the organ donation committee of the Kidney Foundation of Canada, said major religious denominations have closely examined the ethical questions surrounding the removal of organs from brain-dead patients.

11. They have concluded there are no moral problems with such transplants, he said.

"It's essentially the equivalent of decapitation [head cut off]," he said. "It's generally agreed that if a person is decapitated, they are dead."

12. John Dossetor, a leading medical bioethicist, said there's no doubt that a brain-dead patient is dead. He referred to a case documented in medical journals that he said is "extreme" but that, nonetheless, drove home his point. A pregnant woman suffered brain death, but her doctors kept her on life support for 10 weeks and delivered a live infant.

13. After the plug was pulled and an autopsy was performed, the woman's skull was opened and there was nothing but water inside. The brain had liquified and the coroner could see right into the spinal column, Dossetor said.

14. This example, however, did not satisfy John Yun, a cancer specialist, who also testified against transplants.

"I Was Wrong"

15. Dr. Yun said he worked in a busy trauma hospital a decade ago and kept brain-dead patients on life support for organ transplants. Now, after reflecting on the ethics, he thinks he was wrong.

"The problem started when I began to think about the life of the donor. I assumed that the donor was dead. Once dead, no one will object to any way we dispose of the body, so long as it is respectful. But now I believe those patients I looked after in ICU were alive."

16. Yun said he now realizes the whole concept of brain death was created with one aim in mind—organ harvesting. "We must not jump to the conclusion that a doubtful definition of death—the medical hypothesis of brain death—is, in fact, death."

17. Yun said he doesn't believe someone is dead if just one organ—even if it is a crucial one—is dead.

"Is the seed of the soul the brain? That is where my question begins."

SCANNING FOR IMPORTANT INFORMATION: UNDERLINING

Underline the answers to the following questions.

Government Health Committee

1. What was the purpose of the committee?
2. What experience did Ruth Oliver have?
3. Why are more and more philosophers and churches rejecting brain death?
4. What was the situation before 1968, and what is the situation now?
5. Why does Michael Brear disagree?

No Moral Problem

1. What is the position of major religious denominations according to Rabbi Reuven Bulka?
2. What does he compare being brain dead to?
3. Why was the woman kept on life support for 10 weeks?
4. What condition was her brain in after these 10 weeks?

"I Was Wrong"

1. What was John Yun's position 10 years ago?
2. What is it now?
3. Why does he think the concept of brain death was created?

Conclusion

On what idea does Dr. Yun build his position?

Compare what you underlined with your partner. Try to agree on what you think is important information. Make any changes that are necessary.

Recapping the Information: Note Taking

Fill in the following outline using only the information you underlined. Use your own words as much as possible.

Main Ideas	Details
A. Health Committee	
purpose of committee	_____
	_____
issue raised by doctors	_____
	_____
Ruth Oliver's experience	_____
	_____
	_____
prior to 1968	_____
now	_____
Michael Brear	_____
B. No Moral Problems	
position of major denominations	_____
	_____
reason for position	_____
example of pregnant woman	_____
C. "I Was Wrong"	
position 10 years ago	_____
position now	_____
reason for change	_____
	_____

opinion why concept
of brain death created _____

_____

D. Conclusion
Dr. Yun's basic
question _____

Use your notes to talk about the article to each other. Make sure you use complete sentences and explain as much as possible.

REACTING TO THE INFORMATION

Find these quotes and discuss them with your partner. Use the context in which they appear

1. "The so called 'beating-heart cadavers' who are used as donors are, in fact, living patients. They are sick, they are dying. They are living and not dead."
2. "It is essentially the equivalent of decapitation. It's generally agreed that if a person is decapitated, they are dead."
3. "Is the seed of the soul the brain? That is where my question begins."

■ After Reading

RETELLING THE INFORMATION

■ **TIP:**
It is very helpful for the listener if you mention the main ideas and then go back and talk about each main idea in detail.

Work with a partner who took notes about the other story. Use your notes to retell the information. Explain the ideas clearly in your own words. Encourage your partner to ask questions about the information or write some of the important facts you explain.

DISCUSSING THE INFORMATION

1. Together, discuss the quotes in "Reacting to the Information." Try to give an opinion on each other's reading.

2. Go back to the agree/disagree statements on pages 217–218. Talk about them again and see if you still hold the same opinion.

APPLYING THE INFORMATION: MAKING A DECISION

You are on a committee that has to decide who gets the next available organ. A liver has become available. Using all three readings as well as any ideas of your own, decide who among the following should get this liver.

A. A single mother with three children under the age of twelve. She is thirty years old and was a heavy drinker until a year ago.

B. A fifteen-year-old boy who has already had a liver transplant that was not a success.

C. A sixty-five-year-old woman who has two sons and six grandchildren. She has been the principal caregiver for three of those grandchildren since their parents were killed in a car accident two years ago.

D. A fifty-year-old man whose condition is not as serious as the first three people. He can wait for at least another year. However, he is the father of the woman who just died and whose liver has become available.

▌ Vocabulary Building

EXPRESSIONS IN CONTEXT

English, like many other languages, has some common expressions. These expressions are best understood when read in context. Use the following contexts to find the meaning of the *boldface* expressions. Explain each in your own words.

1. After the **plug was pulled** and an autopsy was performed, the woman's skull was opened and there was nothing but water inside.

_____

2. He referred to a case that he said is "extreme" but that, nonetheless, **drove his point home**.

_____

3. "I figured we'd **carry her** as long as possible, and when the time came, we'd get her a heart-lung transplant".

_____

4. In 1994, Patti **set her sights** on getting a degree as a surgical assistant.

_____

5. There is heated debate about whether prisoners deserve a **spot on the list**.

_____

Check your answers with a partner or with your teacher.

Practice using these expressions by putting each into a sentence of your own.

1. _____

2. _____

3. _____

4. _____

5. _____

USING QUOTES

In English, quotes are almost always used to support a point that has already been made.

Example: In paragraph 1 of the article "His Daughter's Gift of Life," the quote "Without you, there wouldn't be any people like me" is used to support the idea that Szuber is thanking the relatives of organ donors.

In your own words, write the points that the following quotes support.

1. _____

"Medical people tell me that they can speak all they want about donation, but until you have somebody who has experienced it, it does not have the impact." (paragraph 2)

2. _____

"I had kind of given up, I had waited so long." (paragraph 3)

3. _____

"I didn't think it was right. And I wasn't sure I could stand every heartbeat reminding me of Patti." (paragraph 4)

4. _____

"He was fine physically, but he was emotionally upset." (paragraph 5)

5. _____

"It's hard to celebrate a life and death at the same time, so we just kind of forget about it." (paragraph 5)

6. _____

"I pray every morning and night and I keep thanking God for this miracle." (paragraph 6)

Check your answers with a partner. Refer to the reading if necessary.

Expanding Your Language

SPEAKING

A. Debate: "The selling of organs will help solve the problem." Debate the preceding statement, using the following steps as a guide.

1. Choose the side you will argue.
2. Make a list of ideas in support of your position.

3. Work with a partner arguing the same position and add to your list of ideas.

4. Divide the ideas between you and decide what each person is going to say.

5. Predict what the other side will say and prepare to "attack" their ideas.

6. Practice your arguments.

7. Present and argue your position against a pair who prepared the other side.

B. Exploring the Possibilities: Given that one day in the future we might be able to do the following things, discuss the implications of each.

1. Transplant a brain in order to treat people who have suffered a stroke or who have a mental disease.

2. Transplant a whole body in order to treat people who are paralyzed from the neck down or who for other reasons cannot move or feel.

Consider points such as these in your discussion:

- If John's brain goes into Mary's body will the result be Mary or John?

- If a 75-year-old gets the body of a 20-year-old and lives for another 60 years, does that make him 135 years old? Or has he died and been brought to life again?

WRITING

Reaction Writing: Continue writing in your journal. Focus on ideas that you really agree with as well as ideas that you really disagree with.

Free Writing: Write about the following.

- What do you think life is?

- Can life be associated with a particular part of the body—for example, the brain?

- When can a person be considered dead?

CHAPTER 12

Having Babies

Chapter Openers

Think about these questions. Share your ideas with a partner or with a small group.

1. Is it important to be able to have children? Why? Why not?
2. Should there be a minimum or maximum age for having babies? If yes, what should the limits be? If not, why not?
3. Why are some people unable to have children?
4. What methods are now available for people who cannot have children normally? List as many as you can think of.
5. Discuss any drawbacks that these methods might have.

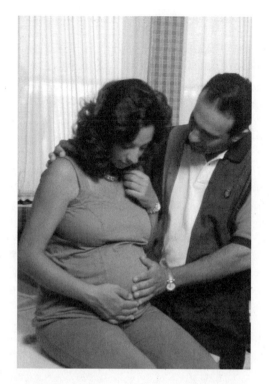

MATCHING MEANING

Match the word in Column A with the definition that best matches it in Column B.

Column A

_____ 1. menopause

_____ 2. surrogate mother

_____ 3. hormones

_____ 4. procreate

_____ 5. fertilization

Column B

a. making egg cell capable of developing into complete organism

b. to produce children

c. time at which woman stops getting her period

d. substances in body that control various processes

e. a woman who has a baby for another woman

FOLLOWING A PROCESS: FERTILIZATION AND HOW IT HAPPENS

Read the following paragraph and use it to fill in the names of the different parts in the diagram that appears after it.

*The two main players in the process of fertilization are the **egg** and the **sperm**. The **egg** is produced by the female and the **sperm** by the male. The female reproductive organs are very simply the following: the **vagina** leading into the **uterus** which is attached to two **ovaries** through the **fallopian tubes**. At birth, a female has between 200,000 and 400,000 **eggs** in her **ovaries**. By the time she reaches sexual maturity, that number will have gone down to about 10,000. Of those, about 400 will be released at the approximate rate of one every 28 days. If the **egg** is not fertilized by a **sperm**, it will die and be washed out of the body. Before a **sperm** fertilizes an **egg**, several things must happen. First, the **sperm** must make its way from the **vaginal canal** through the **uterus** and enter the **fallopian tube**. There, in the widest part of the **tube**, it must meet a mature egg that has been released from the **ovary**. When a single **sperm** enters an egg, the fertilized **egg**—which is now called a **zygote**—continues its development and becomes a multicelled ball called a **blastocyst**, which will eventually become attached to the wall of the **uterus**. Two weeks after fertilization, the **blastocyst** develops into an embryo.*

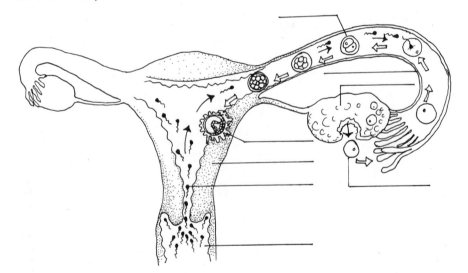

Exploring and Understanding Reading

WHAT IS YOUR OPINION?

Not all women have eggs that can be fertilized. They need to use eggs donated by someone else. Read the following statements and check (✔) the one you agree with the most. Be ready to support your choice.

_____   Egg donation should not be allowed.

_____   Eggs should be donated for free.

_____   Eggs should be donated for a fixed price.

_____   Eggs should be auctioned (sold for the highest price).

Work with a small group of students. Discuss the reasons for your choice.

PREDICTING

The next reading is about young women donating their eggs in order to enable other women to have babies. What do you think you will find out from this reading? List four ideas.

1. _____

2. _____

3. _____

4. _____

Share your ideas with a partner or with a small group.

SURVEYING

Read the introduction and the first sentence of every paragraph after that. Add to or change your prediction statements.

Egg Heads

By Kathryn Jean Lopez

Young women in need of cash are increasingly deciding to sell their bodies

1. Filling the waiting room to its capacity and spilling over into a nearby conference room, a group of young women listen closely and follow the instructions: "Complete the forms and return them, with the clipboard, to the receptionist." It's all just as in any medical office. Then they move downstairs, where the doctor briefs them. "Everything will be pretty much normal," she explains. "Some women complain of skin irritation. You also might be a little emotional. But that is basically it."

2. This is not just another medical office. These girls in their twenties are attend-ing an orientation session for potential egg donors at a New Jersey fertility clinic specializing in in-vitro fertilization. Within the walls of IVF New Jersey and at least two hundred IVF clinics through-out the United States, young women are answering the call to give "the gift of life" to infertile couples. Egg donation is a quietly expanding industry, changing the way we look at the family, young women's bodies, and human life itself.

3. It is not a pleasant way to make money. Unlike sperm donation, which is over in less than an hour, egg donation takes the donor some 56 hours and includes several tests, ultrasound, self-administered injections, and retrieval. Once a donor is accepted into a program, she is given hormones to stimulate the ovaries, changing the number of eggs matured from the usual one per month up to as many as fifty. A doctor then surgically removes the eggs from the donor's ovary and fertilizes them with the designated sperm.

4. Although most programs require potential donors to undergo a series of medical tests and counseling, there is little indication that most of the young women know what they are getting themselves into. They risk bleeding, infection, and scarring. When too many eggs are matured in one cycle, it can damage the ovaries and leave the donor with weeks of abdominal pain. (At worst, complications may leave her dead.) Longer term, the possibility of early menopause raises the prospect of future regret. There is also some evidence of a connection between the fertility drugs used in the process and ovarian cancer.

5. But it's good money—and getting better. New York's Brooklyn IVF raised "donor compensation" from $2,500 to $5,000 per cycle earlier this year in order to keep pace with another clinic nearby. It's a bidding war. "It's obvious why we had to do it," says Susan Lobei, Brooklyn IVF's assistant director. Most New York-area IVF programs have followed suit. Some infertile couples and independent agents are offering even more. The International Fertility Center in Indianapolis, Indiana, for instance, places ads in the *Daily Princetonian* offering Princeton girls as much as $35,000 per cycle. The National Fertility Registry has an online catalogue for couples to browse in, and advertises $35,000 to $50,000 for Ivy League eggs. While donors are normally paid a fixed rate per cycle, there have been reports of higher payments to donors who produce more eggs.

6. College girls are the perfect donors. Younger eggs are more likely to be healthy, and the girls themselves frequently need money—college girls have long been open to classified ads offering to pay them for acting as guinea pigs in medical research. One 1998 graduate of the University of Colorado set up her own Web site to market her eggs. She had watched a television show on egg donation and figured it "seemed like a good thing to do"—especially since she had spent her money during the past year to help secure a country-music record deal. "Egg donation would help me with my school and music expenses while helping an infertile couple with a family." Similar advertisements are scattered throughout the Web.

7. Defenders argue that it's only right that women are "compensated" for the inconvenience of egg donation. Brooklyn IVF's Dr. Lobel argues, "If it is unethical to accept payment for loving your neighbor, then we'll have to stop paying baby sitters." As long as donors know the risks, says Mark McGee of the University of Pennsylvania's Center for Bioethics, this transaction is only "a slightly different version of adoption."

8. Not everyone is enthusiastic about the "progress." Egg donation "represents another rather large step in turning procreation into manufacturing," says the University of Chicago's Leon Kass. "It's the dehumanization of procreation." And as in manufacturing, there is quality control. "People don't want to admit it, but there is . . . the notion that you can have the best eggs your money can buy," observes sociology professor Barbara Katz Rothman of the City University of New York.

9. The demand side of the market comes mostly from career-minded women, the feminists, who thought they could "have it all," a job and a family. Indeed they can have it all—with a little help from some younger eggs.

10. Unfortunately, the future looks bright for the egg market. Recently, a woman in Atlanta gave birth to twins after she was implanted with frozen donor eggs. The same technology has also been successful in Italy. This is just what the egg market needed, since it avoids the necessity of coordinating donors' cycles with recipients' cycles. Soon, not only will infertile couples be able to choose from a wider variety of donor offerings, but in some cases donors won't even be needed. Young women will be able to freeze their own eggs and have them thawed and fertilized once they are ready for the intrusion of children in their lives.

11. There are human ovaries sitting in a freezer in Fairfax, Virginia. The Genetics and IVF Institute offers to cut out and remove young women's ovaries and cryopreserve (preserve by freezing) the egg-containing tissue for future implantation. Although the technology was originally designed to give the hope of fertility to young women undergoing treatment for cancer, it is now starting to attract the healthy. "Women can wait to have children until they are well established in their careers and getting a little bored, sometime in their forties or fifties," explains Professor Rothman. "Basically, motherhood is being reduced to a good leisure time activity."

–National Review

ANALYZING THE INTRODUCTION

A. Read the first two paragraphs again. Highlight the section in which the author

_____ indicates that the clinic is an IVF clinic.

_____ focuses on what aspect of egg donation she will discuss.

_____ describes a general clinic scene.

Number the preceding topics according to the order in which they appear.

B. Point of view. Read the following statements. Check one and be prepared to support your choice.

The author believes that the egg donation industry

- will have no impact on society.
- will have some impact on society.
- will have major impact on society.

Compare your answers with a partner.

INFORMATION QUESTIONS (PARAGRAPHS 3–11)

Look for the answers to these questions. Underline the section in the article that supports your answer.

1. What are the three main steps involved in egg donation?

   a. _____

   b. _____

   c. _____

2. What are the possible side effects to the donors?

   Short term

   a. _____

   b. _____

   c. _____

   Long term

   a. _____

   b. _____

3. Why did Brooklyn's IVF raise its "donor compensation"?

_____

_____

4. How much money can be made from egg donation?

_____

5. What two factors combine to make college girls the perfect donors?

a. _____

b. _____

6. Where does most of the demand come from?

_____

_____

7. Give two examples of the latest advances in the egg market

a. _____

b. _____

Check your answers with a partner. Refer to what you have underlined if you do not agree.

ANALYZING QUOTES

■ *READING TIP:*
Quotes are some-times used to present different opinions.

The author presents two opposing positions with respect to donor compensation and uses quotes for support. Find two quotes that agree with the idea of giving money to the donor and two that are against.

FOR   AGAINST

1. _____   1. _____

_____   _____

2. _____   2. _____

_____   _____

For both positions, think about the following questions.

- What is egg donation being compared to?
- What kind of feeling is it associated with?

Share your answers with a partner. Decide which position is stronger. Why?

EXAMPLES: SUPPORTING A POINT OF VIEW

The author gives the following examples at the end of the article to show that egg donation is changing the way in which we look at the family. Choose one of the examples. Work with a partner who has chosen the same one.

A. Skimming/Highlighting: Read the example you chose and highlight:

- The characters involved
- What they are fighting over
- The result

Example 1

John and Luanne Buzzanca had tried for years to have a child. Finally they had to go for reproductive technology. An embryo was created for them, using sperm and an egg from unknown donors, and implanted in a surrogate mother. One month before the baby Jaycee was born, John filed for divorce. Luanne wanted child support from John, but he refused. After all, he's not the father. Luanne argued that John is Jaycee's father legally. At this point the surrogate mother, who had agreed to carry a baby for a stable two-parent household, decided to sue for custody.

Jaycee was nicknamed "Nobody's Child" by the media when a California judge ruled that John was not the legal father nor Luanne the legal mother (neither one was genetically related to Jaycee, and Luanne had not even borne her). Enter Erin Davidson, the egg donor, who claims the egg was used without her permission. The sperm donor also jumped in, saying that his sperm was used without his permission. Later, an appeals court gave Luanne custody and decided that John is the legal father, making him responsible for child support. For Jaycee's first three years on earth, these people have been fighting over who her parents are.

Example 2

Complete the activity on Exercise Pages E-7 and E-8.

B. Pair Work: Tell back. Tell each other the story, using the high-lighted information.

C. Pair Work: Retell. Get together with someone who read a different example. Quickly tell your partner about the characters and the area of conflict. Ask your partner to first guess what the final result is before you end the story.

D. Discuss the following:

Do the examples support the author's point?
Which example is more effective? Why?

After Reading

REACTING TO THE INFORMATION

Work with a partner or in a small group. Look at the statements presented on page 243 and answer the following.
Do you still agree with the choice you made?
If not, choose another position and give reasons.
Which statement would the author of the article "Egg Heads" choose? Why?

Refer to the reading to support your answer.

APPLYING THE INFORMATION: EXPLORING THE CONSEQUENCES

A. Late Life Pregnancies. One of the consequences of advances in reproductive technology is that women can have babies at almost any time they want. Work with a partner and discuss the advantages and disadvantages of that.

B. Evaluating Reasons. Do you agree with Professor Barbara Katz Rothman that one reason for having babies at a later age is boredom? Is it a valid reason?

List a few other reasons you can think of. One has been given as an example.

1. *Remarriage* _____

2. _____

3. _____

SKIMMING

The following article is about a grandmother, Cheryl, who wanted to have a baby. Read the article quickly to find out why she wanted a baby and why other people want babies late in life.

SCANNING/HIGHLIGHTING

Read the article again and highlight the following:

- Background information on Cheryl and her husband
- The process she went through
- The result

THE PHILADELPHIA INQUIRER

Beating Nature's Clock

Reproductive technologies force us to rethink who is too old to have a baby.

By Marie McCullough

1. Cheryl and Bob Fillippini met at a charity fund-raiser. A week later, he proposed. She demurred for a couple of months, then they got married, congratulated by her seven children and five grandchildren and his three children.

2. She was 46 and he was 45, old enough to have wrinkles and gray hair, young enough to enjoy adventure and change. He had recently moved to this central California coastal town and was a welder for the school district. She was in law school, a lifelong dream. Like any newlyweds, they reveled in romance, sometimes popping over to Lake Tahoe for a weekend.

3. Only gradually did they realize they wanted to have a baby. They never dreamed that at age 50, with the help of high technology fertility treatment, Cheryl would become one for the books, material for supermarket newspapers. "World's oldest mother of quadruplets," the headlines read.

4. Cheryl and Bob decided to use IVF (in vitro fertilization)—in which the eggs are fertilized in vitro (a lab dish).

5. Thus began an $8,000 investment in injections, blood tests, ultrasounds and extracting eggs out of her ovaries. Even with drugs, Cheryl ripened only ten eggs (a young patient she met had fifty-eight). Five were implanted in her uterus.

6. When the process failed, she and Bob began IVF a second time. Once more, she produced ten eggs. Once more, eight fertilized. Ten days later the pregnancy test was positive. Two weeks after that, the ultrasound showed five tiny fetuses.

8. By Cheryl's ninth week, one fetus had died, but at twelve weeks, four fetuses were still growing.

9. The quads were born by Caesarean section at 30.5 weeks—about 8 weeks early. They were small (2 pounds, 4 ounces to 3 pounds, 4 ounces) but strong. Only Rebekah and Amanda needed oxygen. All four were home within five weeks.

10. Amanda, Rebekah, Bobby and Sydney are 20 months old now, and Cheryl proudly notes that she and Bob have not had child-care help, not even in the exhausting early months when the infants seemed to nurse around the clock. "If we had tried to do this (raise quads) with our first kids, we would have been completely devastated." Bob says. "But we don't get stressed out on a lot of things, because we know the answers. It makes it so much easier when you know you're doing the right thing."

11. Until the arrival of new reproductive technology, older women were unable to have children. Now science is removing that upper age limit, challenging our concept of what is old, what is natural, what is right.

12. That is not to say that lots of women want to go through a pregnancy in the autumn of their lives, but there are quite a few who do.

13. Infertility doctors say their patients give many reasons for wanting a baby so late in life. They include the death of a grown child, empty nest anxiety, and remarriage to a younger man who has never had children. There are also women in their fifties who could not overcome lifelong infertility—until now.

14. So is late-life pregnancy "unnatural" or just unusual?

A. Share your ideas about the following questions. Use the information you highlighted to support your answers

1. What kind of parents do you think Bob and Cheryl will make?
2. Which of the reasons given for late-life pregnancy do you agree with? Why?
3. Do you think the author of this article supports late-life pregnancies? Why or why not?
4. One woman's reaction to this article is: "I think one should follow nature, and if nature says it's finished, then it's finished." Would you agree? Why or why not?

B. According to the article "Egg Heads," eggs can be sold for anywhere from $5,000 to $35,000. Discuss the possible consequences of this.

Vocabulary Building

USE OF REPETITION AND SYNONYMS

A. One way of emphasizing an idea is to repeat key words or use similar terms. In the article "Egg Heads," the author wants to show that egg donation is a business. Two words that she uses several times are *pay* and *money*. Read the article quickly and highlight both words every time you come across them. How many times do they appear?

B. Repeating words and using similar terms also help the reader keep track of the ideas being discussed. Read through the article again and make a list of at least eight terms (other than *pay* or *money*) that the author uses. Put the number of the paragraph next to the term.

Term	Paragraph
cash	*subtitle*
sell	*subtitle*
_____	_____
_____	_____
_____	_____
_____	_____
_____	_____
_____	_____

Are there any paragraphs that do not contain a business-related term? Discuss your work with a partner.

LOADED WORDS

Writers do not always state their opinions directly. Instead they use loaded words or phrases that imply how they feel. It is up to the reader to get the message.

Example: In the "Egg Heads" subtitle, "Young women in need of cash are increasingly deciding *to sell their bodies*," the author is comparing egg donation to prostitution and therefore implies that she does not approve.

Read the following statements and underline the loaded words or phrases. Discuss what the author is implying in each case.

- "Basically, motherhood is being reduced to a good leisure time activity."
- Not everyone is enthusiastic about the "progress."
- Unfortunately, the future looks bright for the egg market.
- Although most programs require potential donors to undergo a series of medical tests and counseling, there is little indication that most of the young women know what they are getting themselves into.
- College girls have long been open to classified ads offering to pay them for acting as guinea pigs in medical research.

Expanding Your Language

SPEAKING

Analyzing a Situation: Get together with three or four students. Quickly review Example 1 on page 249 and Example 2 on page 250. Discuss the possible reasons each character had for the demands he or she made. Imagine that you are the jury. Agree on a verdict. Present your verdict to the class and give your reasons.

Reacting to a Specific Situation: Read the following story and find out about a mistake that happened as a result of in vitro fertilization. As you read the story, keep the above examples in mind as well as the following question:

Who has more right to a child—the person who carries it for nine months or the person to whom it is genetically related?

ASSOCIATED PRESS

Misplaced Embryo Case Explored

An embryologist who assisted in the in vitro fertilization of a woman who gave birth to two babies—one white, one black—knew his error caused the wrong embryo to be implanted in the woman but remained silent, according to a state inquiry.

Michael Obasaju was aware he had given Dr. Lillian Nash the wrong embryos for implantation but prepared a second batch with correct embryos rather than stop the procedure.

The case became public when Robert Rogers and Deborah Perry-Rogers, a black couple from Teaneck, N.J., claimed that Richard and Donna Fasano, who are both white, were given an embryo that the Rogers had previously stored at the IVF New York Clinic in Manhattan.

Mrs. Fasano gave birth to two boys in December 1998. One, who is white, was her biological child; the black baby is no relation.

The mix-up occurred on April 24, 1998, when Mrs. Fasano and Mrs. Perry-Rogers were in the office for embryo implantation after in vitro fertilization of their eggs. In preparing the embryos, Obasaju separated out four of Mrs. Perry-Rogers' fertilized embryos because they were of a lower grade. Instead of throwing them away, he accidentally placed those embryos into a test tube used for Mrs. Fasano's procedure.

Had he announced his mistake immediately, the embryos could have been washed out, said Diane Mathis, a State Department of Health spokeswoman. But Obasaju didn't admit his error until Nash learned that Mrs. Fasano was pregnant. He did not come forward sooner because he thought the wrong embryos would not grow.

The Fasanos filed a malpractice suit against Nash, Obasaju and another physician, Dr. Dov Goldstein. Court papers said Nash informed both couples of the mistake months before Mrs. Fasano gave birth to the boy. The Fasanos did not know the Rogers until they filed suit seeking custody of the black baby.

The Fasanos have said they will give the Rogers custody of the black baby if DNA tests show they are the baby's genetic parents.

Work with a partner. Recount the details of this story to each other.

Do you agree with the custody decision?

Brainstorm two more questions or issues that this article raises in your mind. Share your ideas with the class.

Reacting to the Whole Situation: Get together with four or five students. Discuss the following statements:

- Reproductive technology should be stopped until better regulations have been set.
- Adoption should replace reproductive technology entirely.

WRITING

Reaction Writing: Write your reactions to the ideas that you read about in this chapter. Focus on the different issues that have been raised.

Opinion Writing: Your friend has asked you whether it is better to use reproductive technology or to use adoption. Before you write your response, make an outline as follows:

- Choose a position.
- Think of three reasons for this position.
- Write them out in point form.
- Think of examples or explanations for each reason.
- Write them out in note form.

Now write your opinion, which should consist of the following:

- A short introduction (three or four sentences), of which the last sentence states your point of view
- One paragraph for each reason (eight to ten sentences)
- A short conclusion (one or two sentences)

Give your writing to your teacher for feedback.

Read On: Taking It Further

MAGAZINE ARTICLES

Find an interesting magazine article about some aspect of new advances in medicine. You could look for an article about new developments in cancer research, reproductive technology, organ transplants, or even the use of animals for research. Try to find an article that is no more than two pages long.

Prepare to present the information to a partner or to a small group.

Follow these steps:

1. Skimming: Quickly read the article to get the general idea and to check if the information is interesting.
2. Surveying: Read the introduction (one or two paragraphs) and the first sentence of every paragraph after that.
3. Find the writer's point of view and the ideas he or she uses to support it.
4. Highlight the important information for each idea. Make notes from your highlighting.
5. Practice your presentation.
6. Make your presentation.

READING JOURNAL

Write your reactions to the article in your reading journal. You can also include your reactions to articles presented by your fellow students.

Exercise Pages

Unit 2: Fun Matters

Chapter 3. Extreme Sports

INTERVIEWING

Give yourself 1 point each time your answer agrees with the key.

Key: 1. F 2. F 3. T 4. T 5. F 6. T 7. T 8. F 9. T 10. F
11. T 12. F 13. T 14. T 15. F 16. T

13–16: extremely comfortable with high-risk situations
9–12: fairly comfortable with high-risk situations
5–8: fairly uncomfortable with high-risk situations
1–4: extremely uncomfortable with high-risk situations

Unit 2: Fun Matters

Chapter 4. Taking a Break

GETTING INFORMATION FROM A CHART

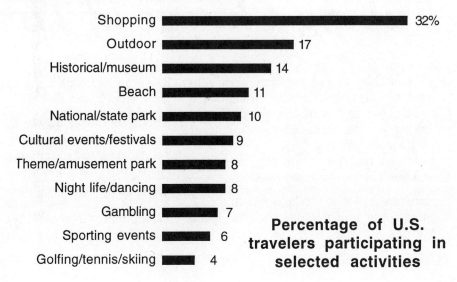

Activity	Percentage
Shopping	32%
Outdoor	17
Historical/museum	14
Beach	11
National/state park	10
Cultural events/festivals	9
Theme/amusement park	8
Night life/dancing	8
Gambling	7
Sporting events	6
Golfing/tennis/skiing	4

Percentage of U.S. travelers participating in selected activities

Unit 3: Time Matters

Chapter 6. Procrastination: Can We Manage Our Time?

GIVING ADVICE: LOOKING FOR TIPS

Prepare to report on the tips you find in the reading. To do this, follow these steps:

1. Skim the article and highlight the tips you find.

2. Make a list of some of the tips.

   _____

   _____

   _____

   _____

   _____

Taking Charge of Time

By Ross Laver

To learn how to use her time more efficiently, Mary-Ann Merrick enrolled in a two-day course. Her instructor was Harold Taylor, a time-management consultant whose book, *Making Time Work for You,* has been translated into five languages and published in fourteen countries.

Here are a few of Taylor's tips and how they made a difference for Mary-Ann Merrick:

Toss out as much correspondence and paperwork as possible.

There's no faster way to increase productivity than to get organized. Start by emptying the in-basket and ending the "pack-rat" syndrome. "I find it works best when I clean out my files every so often and get rid of everything that doesn't belong there," Merrick says. "When correspondence comes in, I file it immediately or make sure it gets done by the end of the week. It keeps me from falling further behind."

Keep a log of your telephone calls.

Making notes when you're on the phone eliminates forgotten messages and follow-ups. It also creates a record that you can refer back to when things go wrong. For example, says Merrick, "I always keep a log when I phone someone to say I've done something. That way they can't call later and say I didn't do it. It's a good way to avoid misunderstandings."

Schedule "appointments with yourself" to complete priority work.

Blocking off time in your daily planner for specific projects reduces the risk that you'll be thrown off your schedule by someone else's lack of planning. Says Merrick: "I use a week-at-a-glance planner and book appointments with myself to do the things I really need to get done each day. That way, when someone asks if I have time to meet with them, I can say, 'Well, I'm busy then but this time is free.'

If you leave your schedule wide open, anything goes."

To avoid interruptions when you're on the phone, turn your back to others.

When your days are filled with interruptions, it's essential to concentrate on one task at a time. A useful trick is to have your phone in a position where your back is to the door. "I like this one a lot. When someone walks in, they can't make eye contact and distract me from my conversation," Merrick explains.

Say "no" more often.

Have as much respect for your own time as for others'. "At first, you feel really guilty saying no, but I've tried it and it works," Merrick says. "Recently, someone asked me to join a new work team. I wanted to help, but if I say yes to everyone, I won't have time to do what really needs to get done." And by focusing on her priorities, Merrick finds that she can accomplish more—with less stress.

–Maclean's

RECAPPING THE INFORMATION

Work with a partner who read the *same information* and compare your list.

RETELLING THE INFORMATION

Work with a partner who read *different information*.

Together, use your tip list to make a new list that contains the information from both lists. Do not repeat any ideas. Decide the best order for the information in your tip list.

Unit 5: Attitude Matters

Chapter 9. Anger: How to Use It

Quickly read the article. Based on the information, decide if the writer is suggesting that anger harms your health or not. Work with a partner who is reading the same article and discuss your opinion.

■■ ————————

Reading 2: How Ideas Affect Us

Anger Aweigh

Clearing the air may relieve pain

The rabbits ruined this year's lettuce. The neighbors commandeered your parking place. And your manager can't understand why you need to stay home with your sick kids. Say something. If you don't express what makes you mad, your body might.

People who tend to hold in their anger might have it come out in the form of lower-back pain, arthritis pain or other chronic aches, according to a recent piece of research.

Out of 142 people suffering chronic pain, the strongest predictor of who hurt the worst is the degree to which people held in their anger (*Journal of Behavioral Medicine*, vol. 17, no. 1, 1994).

"Unexpressed negative emotions may actually suppress the immune and endocrine systems," says study author Robert D. Kerns, Ph.D., associate professor of psychiatry, neurology and psychology, Yale University. These systems are believed to play a role in dimming the experience of pain. Without them functioning at full force, pain tolerance may be reduced, he says.

Studies haven't been conducted to determine whether pain goes away when people constructively express their anger instead of simmering inside. But dealing effectively with the emotions is a healthy skill to develop whether you're in pain or not.

No one technique works for everyone in dealing with anger, says Dr. Kerns. He suggests that some people can learn to channel their strong feelings from self-help books on assertiveness training. But if you're having trouble choosing a book or want one-on-one advice, a professional therapist can help you learn how to let off steam and maybe relieve some of your aches, too.

–Prevention

RATING YOUR HOSTILITY

The questions on pages 193–194 are excerpted from the much longer test Dr. Redford Williams administers to patients. Responses to 15 questions won't determine whether your hostility level is a health risk, but they can suggest whether you would benefit from defusing hostile thoughts.

Questions 1, 2, 6, 10 and 13 are designed to measure cynicism, which Dr. Williams describes as a "mistrusting attitude" toward people's motives and a tendency to be "constantly on guard" against others' misbehavior. If you answered two or more with the responses in parentheses — 1(B), 2(A), 6(B), 10(A), 13(A) — your cynicism level is high.

Questions 4, 7, 8, 11 and 15 measure anger, the tendency to respond with "anger, irritation or annoyance when faced with life's frustrations." If your answers match two or more of the responses in parentheses — 4(B), 7(B), 8(B), 11(A), 15(A) — your anger level is probably quite high.

Questions 3, 5, 9, 12 and 14 measure aggression, the tendency to express your anger, either physically or verbally. A highly aggressive person would most likely choose the responses in parentheses two or more times — 3(A), 5(A), 9(A), 12(A), 14(B).

Unit 5: Attitude Matters

Chapter 10. Getting Through Life

SPEAKING

Simulation: Role Play

To prepare this simulation, choose to work with others and prepare this situation (or the one on page 211).

Scenario B

Consider the following situation. Read the information and decide what action you would recommend and why. Compare your solution to that of others. Together, write out lines of dialogue to role play the situation and your solution.

You work at a bookstore. You work with someone who always seems to be in a bad mood. The person is sometimes rude when you ask a question, even though he has worked there much longer and knows the store better than you do. This coworker never wants to help you or to let you help. Even though you try to be pleasant and begin conversations, your efforts are ignored. This person even insulted you in front of the other workers in the store. One day you find out that this person is being considered for a new and better job as a manager at the store. The company wants you to give your evaluation of this person as part of the decision-making process. You will be meeting with the head of personnel to give your recommendation. You plan to give this person a terrible evaluation, but before your meeting you overhear a conversation between your unpleasant coworker and his brother. You find out that your coworker's mother is very ill and that he is the sole support of the family—working while he is trying to finish his degree. Your coworker is behind in his school work and may fail his year as a result. What would your evaluation be?

Step 1: Work with your partners and discuss your recommendation.

Step 2: Prepare the lines of dialogue between the following people:

    a. Pleasant bookstore worker
    b. Unpleasant bookstore worker
    c. Unpleasant bookstore worker's brother
    d. Other employees
    e. Personnel director

Step 3: Use your lines to act out the story, but do not memorize the lines. Be creative.

Step 4: Following your role play, ask the class to complete the following evaluation sheet for the personnel director who will recommend the bookstore worker for a promotion or not.

The candidate would be:

———— A. Outstanding in this position

———— B. Good in this position

———— C. Suitable in this position

———— D. Unsuited for this position

After hearing both role plays, discuss the differences and similarities between your evaluations of this unpleasant coworker. Explain the reasons for your decisions.

Unit 6: Health Matters

Chapter 12. Having Babies

EXAMPLES: SUPPORTING A POINT OF VIEW

Work with a partner who has chosen the same example.

Skimming/Highlighting: Read the example quickly and highlight

- the characters involved
- what they are fighting over
- the result

Example 2

In another case, William Kane left his girlfriend, Deborah Hect, fifteen little bottles of sperm before he killed himself in a Las Vegas hotel in 1991. His two adult children (represented by their mother, his ex-wife) fought against Miss Hect's claim of ownership. A settlement agreement on Kane's will was eventually reached, giving his children 80 percent of his estate and Miss Hect 20 percent. Hence she was allowed three vials of his sperm.

When she did not succeed in conceiving on the first two tries, she filed a petition for the other twelve vials. She won, and the judge who ruled in her favor wrote, "Neither this court nor the decedent's [dead person's] adult children possess reason or right to prevent Hect from carrying out the decedent's right to procreate with the woman of his choice."

Answer Key

UNIT 1 Weather Matters

CHAPTER 1: Our Changing Climate: Reality and Risks

C. Compare and Contrast, pages 5–6

NEGATIVE

1. At least 300 people were killed

2. 250,000 people are homeless

3. A heat wave that could ruin the coffee crops

POSITIVE

1. Helped replenish the wildlife in Africa

2. An abundance of food for mammals

3. 1.5 million flamingos have returned to Kenya.

Previewing, page 6

(Sample answers) **1.** Environmental issues that affect the Arctic.   **2.** Scientific studies in the Arctic.   **3.** The effects of the melting on the wildlife.

Getting the Main Ideas, page 10

Paragraph 2. The reasons associated with the ice shrinking

Paragraph 3. The changes the ice has undergone in the last 30 years

Paragraph 4. The impact of an "Arctic meltdown"

Paragraph 6. The rate at which the ice is shrinking according to data from satellites

Paragraph 7. U.S. rates of ice shrinking according to data from submarines

Paragraph 8. Global warming

Understanding Details, page 10

1. T   **2.** F   **3.** T   **4.** F   **5.** T

Presenting Information in Table Form, pages 11–13

Table 1: General Consequences of Freezing Rain

AMOUNT OF RAIN (INCHES)	CONSEQUENCES
0.4	Sidewalks become treacherous
1.2	Small tree branches fall
2.8	Trees and utility poles fall
4.0	Hydroelectric towers can fall

Table 2: People Affected

Number of People

2.9 million	2.4–3.2
0.9 million	3.2–4
185,852	>4.0

Table 3: Damages

Areas	Damages
People	1. 100,000 people had to live in shelters
	2. $10 million was needed for victims
Electric Power	1. 1,000 power transmissions and 30,000 utility poles fell
	2. 1.7 million customers lost electricity
Crops	1. 1/3 of farming land was damaged
	2. 5.3 million sugar maple trees were hit
Dairy	1. 1/4 of Canada's cows were killed
	2. 2.5 million gallons of milk had to be dumped

Skimming, page 13

a. The author does not believe that global warming is as serious as many people think.
b. Correct **c.** Correct **d.** The author recognizes some negative effects, like the dry periods in Asia and California. **e.** Correct

Finding Support for an Argument, pages 16–17

Past

2. Food production surged. **3.** Death rates declined in many places. **4.** Prosperity stimulated an outpouring of creativity – in architecture, art, and practical invention.
Future

5. And with an increase in CO_2, forests all over the world should be more robust, allowing them to support more wildlife. **6.** A modest warming in the normally cold and dry polar regions will actually mean more arctic ice, not less. **7.** Most of the warming if it occurs, will be toward the poles. That means there will be less of a temperature difference between the equator and the poles, which means fewer big storms.

Applying the Information: Making a Decision, page 17

(sample answers)
Beneficial

1. Provides a better physical environment for many animals **2.** Provides an abundance of food for many animals **3.** Increased CO_2 levels
Not beneficial

1. Extreme weather conditions **2.** Many deaths due to those conditions **3.** Negative affect on some animals natural habitats

Reacting to a Point of View, page 18

(sample answers)

1. No. The negative effects, like the changes in weather, El Niño, the change in the polar bear habitat   **2.** No, because there are a lot more environmental factors: high population, higher pollution, different types of toxic gases emitted.   **3.** Too much CO_2 can be dangerous for humans.

Synonyms, page 18

1. d   **2.** e   **3.** b   **4.** f   **5.** a   **6.** c

Vocabulary in Context, page 19

1. great benefit   **2.** increased   **3.** decreased   **4.** allows for more production   **5.** opposing   **6.** people who spread fear   **7.** caused   **8.** large

Speaking, page 20

B. 1. People are causing it to rain because of pollutants they are producing going into the atmosphere.

CHAPTER 2: A SAD Situation

Matching, page 24

1. f   **2.** b   **3.** g   **4.** a   **5.** d   **6.** c

Skimming, page 25

1. In the winter (cold, dark months)   **2.** Depressed

Scanning for Specific Information, page 28

1. a. For attempted suicide.   **b.** Her children's vacation came the first week of March rather than in February.

2. The second patient became more sociable and paid more attention to his personal hygiene.

3. a. sadness, irritability, anxiousness   **b.** They can interfere with personal relationships and they can affect the way people function.

4. laziness, increase in appetite, hypersomnia

5. a. People start getting SAD symptoms as daylight hours begin to decrease.   **b.** The symptoms can last until May (spring).

6. a. Two kinds of light   **b.** The brighter light worked because it resembled sunlight

Recapping the Information: Highlighting, page 29

A. 1. Usually affected during the winter months; normal people simply affected by the light.
2. Both physical and psychological and they include: depression, irritability, increased appetite, laziness, hypersomnia, anxiousness.   **3.** South African study could predict the patients that would develop SAD because of daylight hours; use of bright light more effective in curing patients than dim light because it resembles the sun.

Scanning for Specific Information, pages 32–33

1. Audrey takes amphetamines.   **2.** Between 4 and 8% of people suffer from SAD, but only 0.25% suffer from reverse SAD.   **3.** Audrey speaks to women's groups about her disorder, because women are twice as likely to suffer from seasonal depression.   **4.** Audrey shops at a mall far from her house because it has the dimmest lighting and it will prevent her from becoming very depressed.   **5. a.** Audrey shops a great deal in the winter, so much so that she cannot control her spending.   **b.** Her doctor suggests that she not keep credit cards in her purse. **c.** Her husband's solution is that she keep two accounts, one for when she is manic and one for when she is not.   **6.** Audrey feels that she has become a more patient and gentler person as a result of her condition.   **7. a.** People often try to quiet Audrey when she discusses her condition.   **b.** Audrey's response is that depression in various forms is quite common and therefore should be openly discussed.

Recapping the Information: Highlighting, page 34

A. 1. Occurs in the spring when daylight hours become longer; can be helped with medication; creates a type of mania.   **2.** She has harsh mood changes; she becomes depressed; she becomes excessive once the depression passes; the condition has made her a gentler and patient person. **3.** She discusses it openly; she educates others about Reverse SAD; she has taken a few precautions such as maintaining two bank accounts and not carrying credit cards with her.

Scanning for Details: Reordering Information, page 37

1. c   **2.** a   **3.** e   **4.** d   **5.** b

a. Signal about increased light goes to the internal clock.   **b.** Clock sends information to pineal gland.   **c.** Pineal gland releases lower amounts of melatonin into the blood.   **d.** Body temperature remains the same.   **e.** Energy increases and depression lifts.

Adjectives and Nouns, page 39

1. a. depression (n)   **b.** depressed (adj)   **2. a.** illness (n)   **b.** ill (adj)   **3. a.** warm (adj.) **b.** warmth (n)   **4. a.** Biology (n)   **c.** biological (adj)

Vocabulary in Context, page 40

a. 9   **b.** 5   **c.** 6   **d.** 8   **e.** 4   **f.** 2   **g.** 1   **h.** 3   **i.** 7

UNIT 2 Fun Matters

CHAPTER 3: Extreme Sports

Quotations, page 46

1. For   **2.** For   **3.** Neutral   **4.** For   **5.** Against   **6.** Neutral

Previewing, pages 50–52

B. 1. Fearless, like danger, determined, dedicated, love of life   **2.** They all feel very good about what they do and they are all passionate about their respective sports.   **3.** They incorporate their fear into their actions and they all realize that fear is an unavoidable element of their sports.

Predicting, page 52

(sample answers)

1. Risks   **2.** Extreme Sports   **3.** Injuries   **4.** Trends

Scanning for details, page 56

1. 600 feet   66 miles per hour   **2.** BASE stands for: building, antenna, span (bridge) and earth (cliffs).   **3.** snowboarding, ice climbing, skateboarding and paragliding   **4. a.** Participation in snowboarding has grown 113% in the last 5 years. **b.** Baseball and touch football participation has declined.   **5.** Americans today want to participate in sports which have a greater risk factor and push them to their personal limits.   **6.** The activities that are becoming popular are all more challenging than a game of football.   **7.** As a result of paragliding, Mike Carr broke 10 ribs and collapsed his lung.   **8.** He still does it because it has taken over his life and it has a magical quality to it.   **9.** Previous generations faced global wars, childbirth complications, diseases, pandemics, dangerous products, and even threats of mutually assured destruction.   **10.** It is important to have a certain amount of risk in life because it is through risk that new discoveries are made.

Using Evidence to Support Ideas, pages 57–58

IDEA	SUPPORT
2. More Americans are getting hurt.	**a.** 48,000 Americans went to the emergency room for skateboarding accidents.
	b. Snowboarding accidents were up 31%.
	c. Mountain climbing accidents are up 20%.
	d. 46 participants have been killed doing BASE jumps.
3. Americans are not letting injury stop them from taking risks.	The example of Mike Carr
4. In the past, life was full of risk.	**a.** global wars
	b. childbirth complications
	c. diseases
	d. dangerous products
	e. threat of the Cold War
5. For recent generations, the traditional risks have been reduced.	**c.** Americans 57% less likely to die of heart disease than their parents.
	d. smallpox, measles and polio virtually eliminated in the U.S.

6. Everyday risk is minimized, so people look for risk elsewhere.   The example of Joy Marr

Reacting to the Information, pages 58–59

1. c   **2.** d   **3.** a   **4.** b

Scanning/Highlighting, page 63

(sample answers)

1. Alan was very scared, but he kept calm and kept on moving.   **2.** He kept asking the Sherpas if he had enough oxygen to make the climb, focused on making it down alive.   **3.** He was a little disappointed about the mess, but very impressed by the view.   **4.** He learned about teamwork and pushing to the extreme to realize your dreams and that failure is an integral part of success.

Retelling the Information – Making a Profile, page 65

Reasons for climbing: personal success

allows better performance in life in general

teaches how to overcome problems

builds teamwork

Feelings during the climb: nervousness

excitement

exhaustion

fear

Reaction to reaching the summit: humbling

disappointment

feelings of overwhelming joy

sense of accomplishment

How the experience will be used: to help make a greater contribution to the surrounding world.

to apply to experience and the lessons learned to daily life.

to learn that failure is an integral part of success.

to know that dreams can come true.

Using Punctuation – Commas, pages 66–67

1. that his parachute will open facing away from the dam, that his canopy won't collapse, that his goggles will be handy, that no wind will slam him into the concrete   **2.** landing, packing his chute, letting out a war cry   **3.** defiance, thanks, victory   **4.** BASE jumping, snowboarding, skateboarding, ice climbing, paragliding   **5.** danger, skill, fear   **6.** baseball, touch football, aerobics   **7.** smallpox, measles, polio

CHAPTER 4: Taking a Break

Previewing, page 72

(sample answers)

1. the history of vacations   **2.** the effect of technology on vacations   **3.** the future of vacations

Skimming, page 72

2. there was a change in work style.

Note Taking: Understanding Reasons, page 74

MAIN POINTS (TIME PERIOD)	DETAILS (REASONS)
A. Before industrial revolution No real vacation	**1.** Only rich had money & time **2.** Most people were farmers and had to tend their farms all year
B. During and after industrial revolution Vacation becomes more common	**1.** North America turns from agricultural to urban industrial society **2.** Work separated from life **3.** People ruled by the clock
C. Technological revolution No division between vacation and work	**1.** People more available **2.** People work harder to buy more things **3.** People bring cell phones and computers on vacation

Skimming, page 75

1. archeological digs, traditional tours of the country, living on a kibbutz   **2.** students; people interested in archeology, history, and culture; people looking for a different type of vacation

Scanning for Details, pages 77–78

1. 5:45 A.M.   wake up
6 A.M.   start digging in the dirt (already had a snack)
9 A.M.   breakfast break
             lunch and siesta
             lectures and field trips
7:00 p.m.   dinner
9:00 p.m.   bedtime

2. went back to school to study business; allied herself with an Ottawa travel agency   **3.** people interested in history, archeology, or culture; people interested in a different type of vacation
4. good health; able to work in their own garden   **5.** 150 hectares; 5,000 years (3,000 B.C.)
6. taxes, insurance, tips for the guides and bus drivers   **7.** Greece, Italy, Mexico

Note Taking, pages 78–79

MAIN IDEA	DETAILS
B. Origin of the Idea	
Who	Mina Cohn
From	Israel
How started	saw that non-archeologists enjoyed digging but did not know how to join an excavation
C. Trip	
Overall schedule	five or six days working on a dig and the remainder of the trip touring the country with first class accommodations.
Daily schedule	wake up at 5:45, dig starts at 6, breakfast at 9, lunch, siesta, tours and lectures, dinner at 7, bedtime at 9.
D. Excavation site	
Where	south of the Sea of Galilee
How old	5,000 years (3,000 B.C.)
Size	150 hectares
Findings	Roman colonnaded street
	an amphitheatre
	bath house
E. Participants	
Number	15–40
Background	interest in history, archeology, culture, alternative vacation
Requirements	good health
	able to dig in own garden
F. Cost	$2,500 per person from Montreal or Ottawa to Israel
G. Future plans	to start Archaeological Encounters trips to Greece, Italy and Mexico

Skimming, page 80

1. hair care, massages, facials, mud packs and nail services   **2.** people who have little time, but some money; don't need to be rich anymore to go to a day spa

Scanning for Details, page 82

1. She handles both a career and motherhood.   **2.** 1989: 30; 1999: 1,600   **3.** People cannot afford either the time or the money for week-long spas.   **4.** if your physician prescribes spa treatment   **5.** Canyon Ranch day spa at the Venetian Resort-Hotel-Casino   **6.** The quality of day spas varies a great deal; not all live up to their extravagant advertisements.   **7.** that 26 adults given two 15-minute back rubs a week had less stress, were less depressed, performed better on math tests

Note-Taking: Grouping Similar Information, pages 83–85

MAIN IDEA	DETAILS
B. Why popular	wallets are fat, time is slim
Colleen Crowe	does not take a lot of time, can slip off for a few hours
Ronni Burns	does not like too much relaxing so day spa very convenient
Joan Haratani	considers massage and whirlpool an absolute necessity
C. Description/services	
Expensive	
Avon	
Where	New York City's Fifth Avenue
Size	20,000 square feet
Colors	cool shades of celery and dove
Services	haircut, hair color, massages, facials, mud packs, nail services
Venetian Resort	
Where	Las Vegas
Size	16,000 square feet
Pool	private pool filled with flowers
Special room	steam and get covered in mud while looking at a replication of a night sky; fake rain falls to wash the client clean
Other	
Department stores	aromatherapy
Gyms	packing mud
Spa-mobiles	bring services to your home and have teen specials
Home	while you are being pampered some services will even clean your house
Companies	hiring on-site message therapists
D. Types of clients	
Sex	1/4 are men
Salary	1/3 make $45,000 or less a year
Age	half are between 34 and 52

E. Problems/benefits

quality	can vary greatly and all do not meet the extravagant promises of their advertisements
study	26 adults who received two 15-minute back rubs per week lowered their stress, depression and increased their math scores.

Applying the Information: Exploring the Benefits, page 85

(sample answer)

Quality time with family members, exercise and cultural experiences.

Skimming, page 86

Return from vacation with a new perspective on life; gain the will to get through any challenge; develop close relationships with fellow travelers; become more confident in general

Using Quotes, page 88

(sample answers)

1. Jane Wolfberg; looking for ways to bring her experiences into her everyday life, not afraid of trying new things, joined a hunt club.   **2.** Marybeth Bond; gave up the confines of her job to explore the world, redefined her life   **3.** Richard Bangs; did not like what was happening around him, gained a new perspective through adventure travel.   **4.** Melanie Stern; was the type of person who never completed things to the end, now confident that she can do that.

Colors, page 89

TERM	COLOR
Peach	light pink
Petroleum	black
Cream	pale beige
Brick	dark red
Mint	light green

Parallelism, pages 89–91

(sample answers)

A. 1. The technological revolution that we are living in at the present has brought with it cellular telephones, fax machines, e-mail, and the Internet.   **2.** On a two-week trip, participants spend five or six days working on a dig while staying at a nearby kibbutz, and the remainder touring Israel in the comfort of a coach, staying in first-class hotels.   **3.** Hairdressers are rubbing backs, department stores are doing aromatherapy, and gyms are packing mud.   **4.** Thick robes, mineral water and wine, gourmet buffets, fresh flowers and piped-in music are typical features.   **5.** She trekked in the Himalayas, lived with Hmong villagers in Vietnam, even rode camels across the Sahara and elephants in Asian jungles.

B. 1. The advantages of not drinking are saving money, thinking more clearly, being safer on the road, and being healthier.   **2.** Alcohol affects people physically, psychologically, and socially in their relationships with their families.   **3.** With this shampoo your hair will look healthier, be less likely to fall out, and will grow faster.   **4.** Cellular phones have reduced our vacation time, frustrated our families, and increased our stress.

UNIT 3 Time Matters

CHAPTER 5: Are We In a Race Against Time?

Matching Meanings, page 98

1. d   **2.** a   **3.** b   **4.** c   **5.** f   **6.** e

Skimming, page 99

(sample answer) Yes we like to live our lives in the fast lane because it is a status symbol to be extremely busy.

Scanning, page 99

1. He is a writer who wrote a book called *Faster: The Acceleration of Just About Everything.*
2. According to Gleick, we are addicted to speed.   **3.** By multitasking, we are not doing one task as well as we would like to.   **4.** People feel that being too busy is a status symbol.
5. People lead rushed lives because they choose to and they want to see just how far they can push it.

Skimming, page 102

(sample answer) We do not like to live our lives in the fast lane because pauses are an essential part of human life.

Scanning, page 103

1. James Gleick is a science author who wrote a book about speed and its history.   **2.** The people are a particular species, the thirty-somethings.   **3.** Celente feels that if a person is not in contact with him for a short period of time, there will not be any serious consequences.
4. Everyone.   **5.** the Sabbath; stock market pause at the end of the day; pause in the news cycle from evening to morning.

Matching Meanings, page 106

1. e   **2.** d   **3.** f   **4.** a   **5.** c   **6.** b

Skimming, page 106

(sample answer)

The experience of waiting is both positive and negative. Positive because there are good things to wait for: a marriage proposal, the end of school, waiting for Christmas morning. The negative aspects of waiting include bad music and the combined waiting time of five years in a lifetime.

Understanding Descriptive Details, pages 110–111

A. 1. very frustrated, angry.   **2.** North Americans see it as a taking away from life, a waste of time.   **3.** as a type of payment in little chunks of time   **4.** to impress people with how important he is and to remind them who is boss   **5. a.** Louis XIV had to wait a while his royal driver was just arriving at the door.   **b.** In 1949, Joseph Stalin made Mao Zedong wait 17 days in the cold Russian winter before meeting him.
B. 1. a. a weekend   **b.** the Messiah   **c.** the ship to come in   **2. a.** Christmas morning
b. the last day of school   **c.** the end of a car trip   **3. a.** marriage proposal   **b.** results of a pregnancy test   **c.** to give birth   **4. a.** jury to reach a verdict   **b.** in prison   **c.** biopsy results

Understanding Facts and Opinions, page 111

A. 1. O   **2.** F   **3.** F   **4.** O
B. (sample answers) "Americans spend 101,369,863 hours waiting in line." F
      "It is a dreadful sort of idleness, an unbearable tedium to sit motionless like this." O

Word Forms, page 114

A. (sample answers)
NOUN   MEANING

1. researchers   people who conduct research

2. author   person who writes

3. users   people who make use of a service

B.   1. biologist   **2.** depression   **3.** essentially   **4.** naturally   **5.** informative   **6.** insulting   **7.** convenient   **8.** convenient   **9.** tolerant

Vocabulary in Context, page 115

1. hustle   **2.** contemplate   **3.** speculate   **4.** recognize   **5.** boasted   **6.** challenged
7. take over   **8.** dictate

CHAPTER 6: Procrastination: Can We Manage Our Time?

Matching Meanings, page 120

1. b   **2.** c   **3.** a

Understanding Details in a Study, page 123

Report on Procrastination Studies

Background

Purpose of Research: To prove that procrastination is unhealthy

Overall Results of Research: Procrastination causes stress and health problems

Author of Study: Dianne M. Tice and Roy F. Baumeister

Study No.1

Subjects: 44 students in a health psychology course

What information was collected and when: Daily symptom checklist, weekly measures of stress and work requirements for a month

Results: Self-reported procrastinators handed in papers late and got lower marks, others got higher marks.

Study No.2

Subjects: 60 students

What information was collected and when: Not given

Results: Procrastinators have more stress and health problems.

Vocabulary Building, page 127

A. 1. c   **2.** b   **3.** d   **4.** a

B. (sample answers)

IDEA	EXAMPLE
1. Procrastination is a behavior.	drug abuse, impulsivity, poor self-regulation
2. Serious procrastinators have deep problems.	depression, low self-esteem
3. Procrastinators have health symptoms.	cold, flu
4. Research is important for treating procrastination.	testing students

UNIT 4 Technology Matters

CHAPTER 7: Robots – Machines that Can Think and Feel

Personalizing, page 140

(sample answers)

1. clean the house   **2.** walk the dog   **3.** make dinner   **4.** baby-sit

1. convince the children to go to bed   **2.** earn money   **3.** drive the car   **4.** kiss the children goodnight

Skimming, page 140

The robot at the moment is going through a period of unpopularity, but they predict this will change in the future.

Finding the Main Ideas: Chunking, page 147

MAIN IDEAS	PARAGRAPHS
Introduction	1–4
Previous robots	5–12
Recent advances	13–18
Three generations of robots	19–23
Examples of self-guided machines	23–29
Robots and the elderly	30–33
The money aspect	34–39

Getting the Important Information, pages 147–148

1. 5–10 years   **2.** they were single function, very limited in their capabilities   **3.** to see the environment and respond to any changes that happen   **4.** advances in the power of computer chips have enabled researchers to build machines that are capable of thinking on their feet **5.** Three   **6.** self-guided machines   **7.** elderly   **8.** they are very expensive

Scanning: Tracing the Development of an Idea, page 151

■ Breazeal begins studying the process of cognitive development in children.

■ She goes to MIT in 1990 to work on a master's degree in electrical engineering and computer science.

■ Breazeal is fascinated by the robots being built by Rodney Brooks, an MIT professor and innovator of artificial intelligence.

■ She begins thinking about building a robot that focuses on the communication skills she cares about.

■ She designs a special software made up of "drives" and "emotions."

Note Taking: Finding Evidence, page 152

■ Kismet's human-like appearance: big, red rubber lips; fuzzy eyebrows; baby-doll eyes scanning the room; head shaped and sized like a human head.

■ Kismet's baby-like behavior: mood changes when Breazeal enters the room; looks at creator with growing interest; grows tired; likes to play with toys; closes its eyes and goes to sleep; needs constant attention.

■ Breazeal's mother-like behavior: looks straight into Kismet's eyes; talks baby talk to Kismet; plays with Kismet with toys; turns around to take away the constant stimulus; greets Kismet like an infant.

Reference Words, pages 153–154

2. mechanical versions of a real person   **3.** the robotic dog named AIBO   **4.** that there is a future for real robots   **5.** people who work at Sony

Expressions in Context, pages 154–155

(sample answers)

1. The robot was very important in those novels.   **2.** Things changed.   **3.** can make money
4. much better than   **5.** The main goal to reach   **6.** thinking on their own in different environments

CHAPTER 8: The Internet—How Do We deal With It?

Matching, pages 158–159

1. b   **2.** c   **3.** f   **4.** d   **5.** a   **6.** e

Skimming, page 3

b. The Internet is developing very fast and is changing many of the ways we do things.

Recognizing the Main Ideas and Details, page 161

1. M   **2.** M   **3.** D   **4.** M   **5.** D   **6.** D   **7.** D   **8.** M

MAIN POINT	DETAIL
1.The wired age is changing daily routines.	More than 70% log on several times a week just after getting home from work.
2. Online shopping is the fastest-growing Internet sector.	Stocks of companies like Amazon.com and iVillage are soaring.
3. You can have a good time on the Internet.	A rapidly increasing number of Americans play games on the Net.
4. The Internet is affecting television.	19% declare that the Internet is more important to them than watching television.

Using Graphic Information, pages 161–163

1. In 1999, $125 million; in 2000, $274 million   **2.** Between 1999 and 2000, $20 billion; between 2003 and 2004, $40 billion   **3.** Most interested in shopping online are single people.

Predicting, page 164

(sample answers)

■ What are the functions and characteristics of a community center? socialize, bring people together, serve the specific needs of a community

■ In what ways can an Internet auction resemble a community center? many people gathered, similar interests, forum to socialize in

Surveying/Chunking, page 164

MAIN IDEA	PARAGRAPH
How eBay similar to community	3
Makes people feel better	4, 5

Antique dealers	6
Criticism of places like eBay	7
Removing division of geography and class	8, 9
Can find love on eBay	10

Using Main Ideas to Scan for Details, page 167

1. with cashier's checks and money orders.   **2.** allows people to make money, gives them a sense of community, brings people together with similar interests   **3. a.** from her travels over the years   **b.** contact with people   **4. a.** mom-and-pop corner store   **b.** vast warehouse of the superstore   **5. a.** because it was her hobby   **b.** $150,000 a month   **6.** People are honest and decent and eBay displays the goodness of human nature.

Reacting to the Information, page 169

A.   **1.** It replaces human contact, makes relationships anonymous.   **2.** People who are bound to their homes can interact with others, people can make a living, people can meet others with similar interests, people can fall in love, people can make money.

Surveying/Chunking, page 170

MAIN IDEA	PARAGRAPH
Why kids like site	3
Encouraging charity online	4
How to save	5, 6
Critics of these sites	8
Restrictions	10, 11, 12

Using Main Ideas to Scan for Details, page 173

1. a. $100 dollars (paragraph 1)   **b.** $1.3 billion (paragraph 2)   **2.** provides games that teach teens how to save, posts articles about saving money (paragraph 5)   **3.** push kids into impulse buying (paragraph 8)   **4.** 29% (paragraph 9)   **5.** Can put a ceiling on individual purchases, can limit online shopping hours (paragraph 10)   **6.** The sites preselect items suitable for the age group. (paragraph 11)

Recapping the Information: Highlighting, page 174

A.   **1.** Sites are affiliated with many companies, offer wide variety of items; kids can have accounts on the sites, can receive gift certificates.   **2.** Sites teach children how to save money, how to donate to charity, can even open bank accounts on the sites.   **3.** They exploit the children and encourage impulse buying.

Applying the Information: Contrasting Ideas, page 175

The author was looking for a cabin in the deep woods of Maine.

No, she found it in a guidebook.

Expressions in Context, page 177

1.d   **2.** c   **3.** a   **4.** b   **5.** f   **6.** e

Vocabulary in Context, pages 177–178

1. invented   **2.** not able to cash because there is no money in the account   **3.** cheating
4. clothing items   **5.** want   **6.** location

UNIT 5 ATTITUDE MATTERS

CHAPTER 9: Anger: How to Use It

Retelling the Information: Is Anger Useful or Dangerous?

1. a. swearing   **b.** smashing things   **2. a.** heart attacks   **b.** fatal coronary disease
3. a professional therapist   **4.** They have evidence that one aspirin a day lowers risk of heart disease.

Reacting: Comparing Studies

(sample answers)

1. Yes, because anger can lead to deadly health problems.   **2.** channel feelings using self-help books, see a therapist   **3.** Yes; because there are many different techniques for anger management, a person can choose what works best.

Debating the Issues, page 188

B. 3. a. Impulse control lessons   **b.** 3–6 years old; that is when the most rapid physical and mental growth takes place.   **c.** very young children who can hardly speak   **d.** Debate exists as to whether it should be only for children who need it the most or for all children to avoid singling any children out.   **e.** Children now come from families that lead more stressed lives.

Vocabulary in Context, page 191

1. f   **2.** d   **3.** c   **4.** e   **5.** b   **6.** a

The Language of Examples, page 7

1. I, stress-reduction strategies; E, meditation   **2.** I, Anger releases stress hormones; E, adrenaline   **3.** I, familiar nursery school tools; E, puppets, games, books, flash cards   **4.** I, promote conversation about emotions; E, children express feelings through drawing journals

CHAPTER 10: Getting through Life

A. Inference, page 202

1. I   **2.** I   **3.** F   **4.** F   **5.** I   **6.** T   **7.** T   **8.** F   **9.** I   **10.** T

B. Charting Results, page 203

STUDY	AUTHOR	RESULTS
Research with 3,920 college students	Dr. Snyder and his colleagues	Hope in freshmen year an indicator of student's success in college
Research of more than 7,000 men and women	Dr. Snyder	■ 40% are hopeful in technical sense ■ 20% believe they can find the means to achieve their goals ■ 20% have energy but no confidence ■ rest had neither the will nor the way ■ 6 attributes of hopeful people
10-year study of 206 patients	Dr. Beck	Their hopelessness scores were the best indicator of whether they would attempt suicide.
Women viewing cancer video	Dr. Lori Irving	Effect of video stronger on women who had a low-score hopefulness scale

Applying the Information: Achieving Our Goals, page 205

A. 1, 2, 3

Vocabulary in Context, pages 208–209

(sample answers)

1. many different areas **2.** invented a way to appraise **3.** same intelligence **4.** obsessed
5. large **6.** trained

Word Forms: Adverbs, pages 209–210

1. surprisingly, ADJ **2.** scientifically, V **3.** typically, V **4.** fairly, ADJ usually, V
5. necessarily, V

UNIT 6 Health Matters

CHAPTER 11: Transplants

Previewing, page 218

(sample answers)

1. trauma of losing a child **2.** celebration of life **3.** transplant controversies **4.** how the family addressed the situation

Surveying, pages 221–222

PARAGRAPH	MAIN IDEA
3	Szuber's health problems started many years ago.
4	how Patti died

5   the result of the transplant

6   the other people who benefited from Patti's organs

Scanning for Details, pages 222–223

1. He had his daughter's heart after she died in a car accident   **2.** One year old   **3.** She decided to go into the medical field.   **4.** Patti had filled out an organ donor card.   **5.** He was emotionally upset.   **6.** He hunts, fishes, and plays golf.   **7.** The other recipients of Patti's organs gained the most because they were on the verge of death themselves until Patti's organs saved their lives.

Skimming, page 224

1. Demand   **2.** a. no money   b. too sick   c. don't have family support

Recapping the Information: Note Taking, pages 228–229

MAIN IDEAS	DETAILS
A. Ms. Jensen	
background	has Down syndrome
	has a bad heart and lungs
request for a transplant	tried to sign up for a transplant in 1995
response	was rejected sight unseen
	the reason was her low IQ
reaction	she and her friends protested until she got her transplant
result	died of complications
	Stanford no longer turns away the mentally disabled
B. Eliminating	
survey	Of 138,000 people who needed transplants, only 1/4 received them.
Reasons for eliminating patients	
money	hospitals want insurance up front
	racial minorities less likely to receive transplant surgery
too sick	people who have complicated illnesses less likely to get transplant.
family support	need a group of people who can help patients through long and complicated recovery period.
C. Ethical Dilemmas	
alcoholics	should receive transplant if they have not had a drink for at least six months

attempted suicides	usually do not perform transplants, but make exception for teens
prisoners	avoided because might not participate in follow up care
	some argue that prisoners easy to find and to follow
age	as long as the person is generally healthy, transplants will take place.
	some organs have cutoff ages
D. Conclusion	Hospitals make mistakes in choosing their candidates.

Skimming, page 230

1. supply   **2. a.** a health committee   **b.** people who support removing organs from brain-dead patients   **c.** people who oppose removing organs from people who are brain-dead

Recapping the Information: Note Taking, pages 233–235

MAIN IDEAS	DETAILS
A. Health Committee	
purpose of committee	to improve Canada's low rate of organ donation
	mostly heard about the consequences of not getting an organ
issue raised by doctors	removal of organs of people who are "brain-dead" but are actually still alive
	fundamental moral mistake to remove organs from people whose brains are declared clinically dead
Ruth Oliver's experience	suffered from bleeding of the brain after childbirth in 1977
	declared clinically dead
	emerged from her condition
prior to 1968	physicians waited till patient had stopped breathing before removing organs
now	doctors wait till patient is brain-dead
Michael Brear	says that 'beating-heart cadavers' are very much alive
B. No Moral Problems	
position of major denominations	concluded that there are no moral problems with such transplants
reason for position	being brain-dead like decapitation, no longer alive if your head is cut off.
example of pregnant woman	brain-dead woman was pregnant, kept her alive to deliver the baby, at autopsy showed that brain had liquified

C. "I Was Wrong"

position 10 years ago	it was fine to take organs from people who were brain-dead
position now	it was not ethically right because patients were really alive
reason for change	believes that his ICU patients were actually alive
opinion why concept of brain death created	created for organ harvesting

D. Conclusion

Yun's basic question	"Is the seed to the soul the brain?"

Expressions in Context, pages 236–237

1. taken off life support   **2.** made his point   **3.** keep her alive   **4.** made it a goal   **5.** place on the transplant list

Using Quotes, pages 237–238

1. Meeting a donor recipient is often more effective than speaking to a doctor.   **2.** His condition was so bad that Szuber had lost hope.   **3.** Szuber is unsure about receiving Patti's heart.
4. Results after the transplant had been completed   **5.** Szuber's joy for life is overshadowed by his daughter's death.   **6.** The miracle that Szuber was able to have a successful heart transplant

CHAPTER 12: Having Babies

Matching Meaning, page 241

1. c   **2.** e   **3.** d   **4.** b   **5.** a

Predicting, page 243

(sample answers)

1. monetary reasons for donation   **2.** future consequences   **3.** criticism of the practice
4. medical screening

Analyzing the Introduction, page 246

Indicates that the clinic is an IVF clinic; first sentence of second paragraph.

Focuses on what aspect of egg donation she will discuss; last sentence of second paragraph.

Describes a general clinic scene, first sentence of first paragraph.

Information Questions (paragraphs 3–11), pages 247–248

1. a. must be accepted as a donor.   **b.** given hormones to stimulate ovaries   **c.** doctor surgically removes eggs from donor's ovary   **2.** Short term: **a.** scarring   **b.** bleeding   **c.** weeks of abdominal pain   long term: **a.** early menopause   **b.** ovarian cancer   **3.** to keep pace with other clinics in the area   **4.** between $5000 and $50,000 +   **5. a.** Younger eggs are likely to be more healthy.   **b.** College girls are often in need of money.   **6.** The demand comes from career-minded women, who want both job and family.   **7. a.** Women can be implanted with frozen donor eggs.   **b.** Women will be able to freeze their own eggs and have them fertilized once they are ready to bear children.

Analyzing Quotes, page 7

For: 1. "If it is unethical to accept payment for loving your neighbor, then we'll have to stop paying baby sitters."   **2.** this transaction is only "a slightly different version of adoption."

Against: 1. Egg donation "represents another rather large step into turning procreation into manufacturing."   **2.** "People don't want to admit it, but there is…the notion that you can have the best eggs your money can buy."

Examples: Supporting a Point of View; pages 249 and E7–E8

A. Skimming/Highlighting

Example 1—**characters:** John and Luanne Buzzanca (the infertile couple), the surrogate mother, the egg donor, the sperm donor, Jaycee (the baby that was conceived through reproductive technology).   **Fight:** They are fighting over who the legal parents of the child are.   **Result:** The infertile couple was given custody.

Example 2—**characters:** William Kane (deceased man who left 15 vials of his sperm), Deborah Hect (his girlfriend at the time of his suicide), Kane's ex-wife, and his two adult children. **Fight:** They are fighting over the vials of sperm. After three vials had been given to Deborah Hect and twelve to his ex-wife and children, Hect filed for the other twelve vials, because she had not been able to conceive with the first three.   **Result:** She was given the vials because she was "carrying out the decedent's right to procreate with the woman of his choice."

Applying the Information: Exploring the Consequences, pages 250–251

(sample answers)

1. Remarriage   **2.** Financial security   **3.** Stability

Scanning/Highlighting, page 251

Background: Cheryl and her husband Bob got married. They each had children and Cheryl had grandchildren. The couple reveled in their new marriage and decided to have a child.   **Process:** Cheryl went through many medical tests and ripened 10 eggs. They were implanted, but the process failed, so produced 10 more eggs, 8 of which were fertilized.   **Result:** Cheryl gave birth to quintuplets.

Use of Repetition of Synonyms, page 254

A. money, 5 times; pay, 4 times   **B.** buy (paragraph 8), expenses (paragraph 6), compensated (paragraph 7), bidding (paragraph 5), market (paragraph 6), fixed rate (paragraph 5)

Loaded Words, page 255

(sample answers)

"reduced"-is a negative term, "leisure time"-makes activity seem unimportant

Text Credits

p. 7: "Arctic Meltdown," by Margaret Munro. *National Post,* Dec. 4, 1999

p. 11: "Ice Storm Numbers Tell Chilling Tale," by Terrance Wills. *The Montreal Gazette,* Dec. 15, 1998. Reprinted by permission.

p. 14: "What's Wrong With Global Warming?" by Dennis T. Avery. Reprinted by permission from Dennis T. Avery.

p. 21: "People May Drive Weather Patterns," by Steven Strauss. Excerpts from "Cars make rain-makers of us all, study says." Reprinted with permission from *The Globe and Mail.*

p. 26: "Seasonal Affective Disorder," by Gila Lindsley. © 1998 New Technology Publishing Inc. and Gila Lindsley Ph.D.

p. 30: "Sad in the Sunshine," by David Johnston. *The Montreal Gazette,* Mar. 10, 1991. Reprinted by permission.

p. 36: "The Biological Clock," by Gila Lindsley © 1998 New Technology Publishing Inc. and Gila Lindsley Ph.D.

p 53: "Life on the Edge," by Karl Taro Greenfield. *Time Magazine,* Sept. 6, 1999. Reprinted by permission.

pp. 61 and 63: Excerpts from "High Drama," by Jamie Clarke. Reprinted by permission from Jamie Clarke.

p. 73: Adapted from "The Rise and Fall of Vacations," by Felicia R. Lee. *The New York Times,* Aug. 14, 1999. Copyright 1999 *The New York Times.* Reprinted with permission.

p. 76: "Getting Down in the Dirt," by Felicity Dunn. *The Canadian Press.* Reprinted by permission.

p. 81: "A Day at the Spa," by Tamala M. Edwards. *Time Magazine,* Oct. 18, 1999. Reprinted by permission.

p. 86: "Wild at Heart," by Sammantha Dunn. Copyright January 2000 *Shape.* Reprinted with permission.

pp. 100, 102, and 112 "Living in the accelerated lane and loving it," by Kim Painter. *USA Today,* Sept. 13, 1999. Copyright 1999, *USA Today.* Reprinted with permission.

p. 107: "I Could Just Scream," by Peter Carlson. Excerpt from "Playing the Waiting Game." *The Montreal Gazette,* Jan. 29, 2000. © *The Washington Post.* Reprinted with permission.

p. 122: "Probing Procrastination," *Science,* Vol. 278, Dec. 5, 1997. Reprinted with permission from *The Global Weekly of Research Science.* Copyright 1997 American Association for the Advancement of Science.

p. 125: "Help! I'm a Procrastinator," *Essence,* Feb. 1999. This article is a reprint with permission from *ESSENCE* Magazine.

p. 129: "Procrastinate now," by Barbara Brotman. Original title: "Here's Something to Read While You're Not Doing Your Taxes," *Chicago Tribune.* All rights reserved.

p. 133: "A Sentimental Journey," by Micta Ojito. *The New York Times,* Feb. 3, 1998. Copyright 1998 *The New York Times.* Reprinted with permission.

p. 141: "Even Sony's Betting on a Robotic Future," by Bill Husted. *Atlanta Journal.* Reprinted with permission from the *Atlanta Journal* and the *Atlantic Constitution.*

p. 144: "The Robot of the House" from "Brave New Robots. Big Strides in Developing Machines for Household," by John Moran. *The Hartford Courant,* Aug. 5 1999. Copyright *The Hartford Courant.* Reprinted with permission.